WHY I DECIDED TO BE A TEACHER TOO

BEING AN EXTERNAL PARENT, COUNSELOR, MENTOR, ROLE MODEL,

SOMPAUL VICTORY

I dedicate this book to my father Director of NPS School

&

All of the Teachers And Student and their Parents

Contents

Foreword

I am presenting this book to all of my readers from all over
the world
This book is based on being a Good Teacher and a role
model of all the student of the world because a teacher
holds the future of the coming generation.

Author

Sompaul Victory

This is Sompaul Victory the author of this book presenting you the book "Why I Decided to Be a Teacher Too"

CHAPTER ONE

INTRODUCTION

The instructing occupation can be described as the father to all different profession. It is consequently considered as a noble profession, which serves as an engine room for the viability to all different quarter of the nation"s economy

To become aware of his existence as an individual. Citizen schooling as one of the foremost objectives of all spherical education. Full and harmonious improvement of children. Promotion of spiritual, moral, cultural, intellectual and bodily improvement of scholars and in faculty and society.

Classroom is like a universe. The instructor is the solar that should grant mild and electricity to its planets i.e. the students. The solely distinction is, as an alternative of turning into the centre of the stated photo voltaic system, this solar have to make certain to revolve round the planets, make them centre of attention, and rotation, and gaining knowledge of process.

"Teacher Education = Teaching capabilities + Pedagogical idea + Professional capabilities."

Teaching capabilities would consist of offering coaching and exercise in the exclusive techniques, methods and techniques that would assist the instructors to layout and impart instruction, grant suitable reinforcement and habits positive assessment. It consists of tremendous study room administration skills, coaching and use of educational substances and verbal exchange skills.

Pedagogical idea consists of the philosophical, sociological and psychological issues that would allow the instructors to have a sound groundwork for working towards the educating competencies in the classroom. The concept is stage unique and is based totally on the wishes and necessities that are attribute of that stage.

"According to Me, pedagogy is the "It deals with processes of upbringing, teaching, learning, and social and cultural development., or profession of teaching.""

Professional capabilities consist of the techniques, techniques and procedures that would assist instructors to develop in the career and additionally work in the direction of the boom of the profession. It consists of tender skills, counseling skills, interpersonal skills, laptop skills, facts retrieving and administration capabilities and above all lifestyles lengthy gaining knowledge of skills.

CHAPTER TWO

TEACHER

A great nation is build though a teacher in the four walls of a class room.
A teacher's profession is a noble one, it is said Yes, it is a noble one.
I feel it is the basis of all other professions. It is the teacher who creates doctors, scientists, engineers, artist, dramatist, singer, builder and all other professionals.

What is a teacher?

A instructor is a expert who shares their understanding on a unique subject or set of matters with a team of puple in hopes of advancing their knowledge, skills, wondering or standard characters. A trainer can additionally be referred to as an educator or instructor. They provide their college students the equipment to clear up issues via making use of the information and ideas they learned.

What do teachers do?

Teachers create engaging lesson plans, educate students, and develop and nurture their interests in education. They can instruct in various subjects and to different students learning at levels. Teachers' responsibilities include assigning and grading homework, documenting progress and planning instructional activities. Generally, teachers will:

- Produce educational material like assignments, course curriculum, notes or tests.
- Coordinate and gather necessary material for presentations.
- Manage classes to ensure an optimal learning experience for all students.
- Plan educational events and activities.
- Keep the classroom organized and clean. Teachers put away trash or supplies at the end of the day.
- Accommodate the needs of their students by adapting their teaching material. They provide personalized instruction when necessary.
- Organize and attend parent-teacher meetings. Teachers communicate with parents about student progress and answer questions when necessary.
- Encourage students, as well as promote enthusiasm and interactive learning with positive reinforcement.
- Evaluate and document student progress and grade assignments, homework and tests.
- Distribute progress cards periodically.

Teacher salary

A teacher's salary varies depending on regional factors and whether they teach in a private or public school. And sometime they teach for free, without getting support.

Requirements to be a teacher

Generally speaking, particularly if speaking about youth in a public school format, an aspiring teacher will have to meet several requirements that may involve the following:

Education

Teachers need a bachelor's degree in teaching or a relevant field in addition to a teaching credential to teach K-12 in public schools. The specifics required for the credential will vary by region, subjects and the ages of the students for whom the teaching credential is earned. Private learning facilities may or may not have similar expectations as determined by the institution.

University and community college professors will need at the very least master's degree in a related subject, though in some instances a Ph.D. in their teaching area can be required or preferred.

Vocational school teachers mostly need experience to teach.

Certification

It is necessary to obtain certification to teach in K-12 public schools. During the education programs, candidates learn the necessary courses, teaching experience and test preparation to apply for a state teaching certification or license. They can also receive guidance from universities or colleges through certification programs.

Depending on your state requirements and the level or subject you plan to teach, you might have to take one or more tests. Most states require candidate teachers to pass at least one teaching certification exam, such as CTET or STET. It might be necessary to take a core exam on teaching pedagogy, policies and ethics. In some cases, a more advanced teaching exam or subject-specific exams are required to get your license.

Skills

What does a teacher do for a student? In truth, a teacher has the ability to help a student in so many ways. Here are some skills required for a role as a teacher:

- **Excellent communication skills**. Verbal and written communication skills are essential for a teacher because their job involves communicating information. They need to explain things in terms that students understand. As they work with children at different learning stages, they need to create an environment where children can learn, discover and express themselves. It helps them grow.
- **Patience**. Teachers sometimes need to explain the same thing several times to students until they understand. They may also encounter students who demonstrate challenging behaviors in the classroom and need to keep their calm. Some situations with parents or administrators might require patience too.
- **Creativity**. Teachers find exciting and enjoyable ways to teach their lessons and keep students engaged and attentive.
- **Critical thinking**. Teachers must answer questions from students or parents, resolve conflicts and plan their work. All these situations require the ability to find the

adapted resource to solve the problem quickly.
- **Presentation skills and confidence**. Teaching involves a lot of public speaking. They need to stand in front of a class and speak confidently.
- **Organization**. Teachers must create, plan lessons and grade assignments in a limited number of hours. They must also manage paperwork filing and documenting.
- **Content knowledge**. Teachers need to understand the material they teach. They must master teaching techniques and their specific subject. Depending on the level they teach, they might also need to have some technical or computer knowledge.

Work environment for teachers

Teachers normally work at some point of faculty hours with students. They every so often want to attend meetings with different teachers, parents or students before and after school. They normally work in the evenings or weekends to grade assignments and put together lessons.

Some instructors work part-time and others full-time. They usually work 9 months all through the yr and have the summer season off until they educate summer time classes.

Teachers more often than not work indoors, though basic instructors occasionally supervise playgrounds outdoors. Teaching small young people may contain publicity to excessive tiers of noise.

Career paths for teachers

Teachers can evolve in their careers when they gain experience and take additional education. They can become school principals or school administrators. To do so, they need to be certified teachers, have three years of experience and get a master's degree in school administration. Once they are certified as school administrators or principals, they can interview and obtain positions in the school board administration.

Elementary school teachers can become high school or middle school teachers if they specialize in chemistry or math, for instance, with an advanced degree in those areas.

How to become a teacher

If you are seriously considering the prospect of becoming a teacher, to prepare yourself you can follow these five steps below:

1. Get a bachelor's degree

Earn a bachelor's degree in education or teaching from an accredited school. You might need to get a considerable number of college credits in your subject area if you plan to teach higher education levels. For your admission in an education program, schools may require minimum GPA and SAT scores or basic competency exams. For example, you might need to take the PRAXIS Core before proceeding with your degree in education.

2. Obtain practical training

You may participate in supervised teaching during your studies and after you get your degree. You will learn to manage the classroom, identify student levels, and identify cultural and societal influences on the learning process. You will also regularly produce reports on your training to your university. Make sure that your university approves the school in which you do your supervised teaching. There are training programs for career-changers who can then get a teacher certification.

3. Pass required exams

You need to fulfill testing requirements according to the school and subject you choose. If you're going to teach a specific topic or in advanced grades, you need to pass exams in that subject. Education-competency exams, may also be required.

This assessment consists of having future teachers self-assess their classroom performance.

4. Get a state teaching license

Teaching licensure requirements vary depending on the state you live in. Inform yourself about those conditions before you start your degree program.

5. Get a master's degree

After becoming a certified teacher, you may want to continue your education and pursue graduate studies. For particular fields, like special education, you need to obtain a master's degree before getting certified in some states.

CHAPTER THREE

GOOD TEACHER

Should the characteristics of a excellent trainer be described totally via pupil achievement? Or ought to they embody characteristics greater challenging to measure -- such as the ability to join emotionally with children?

We observed 6 key behaviours that make a brilliant trainer -- and described specific, actionable approaches to practice these behaviours in the classroom. Start trying out them with your students to stimulate a extra exciting, dynamic, and enticing ride in your coming lessons!

A good teacher instills confidence

In the book *50 Ways to Improve Student Behavior*, middle school teacher Todd Whitaker highlights low student confidence as one of the most persistent obstacles to the success of any teacher. He breaks down a worrying trend:

Many students do not believe that their teachers actually believe in them

Many students do not believe that their parents actually believe in them

Many students do not believe that any adult actually believes in them

Many students, therefore, do not believe in themselves

Students who do not believe in themselves tend to have more behavioral and academic problems

If the final point's conclusion is obvious, the inverse should be just as clear: If students who don't believe in themselves have issues in the classroom, those who do believe in themselves will be better-equipped to succeed academically.

Teacher abilities to build student confidence

Make gaining knowledge of goal-oriented -- If you set described desires with your students -- at the starting of the faculty yr or even of every lesson -- the entire category will have a higher grasp of its man or woman and collective accomplishments. To make studying greater goal-oriented, make decisive statements about the day's mastering goals. For example, begin a lesson with a declaration such as "today you will study the first step of multiplication," and end the type by using saying, "Congratulations! Now you're geared up to exhibit your dad and mom you're mastering how to multiply!" Cultivating this standpoint helps college students take self belief from their very own progress, boosting mastering effects and motivation.

Instill a boom mind-set -- According to psychologist Carol Dweck, a constant attitude conceives of pupil abilities as inflexible and inflexible. In contrast, a increase mind-set views scholar studying as fluid and changing, and pursuits to boost children's competencies and skills via effort and persistence. The boom mindset, Dweck notes, helps college students come to be greater receptive to classes and feedback. While the important points of the pedagogy can be subtle, a few frequent methods to instill a increase attitude consist of moves as easy as encouraging college students to amplify their solutions extra constantly or the usage of success folders.

Reassure your students verbally -- As basic trainer Todd Whittaker argues, if you desire a scholar to consider in himself, "then absolutely inform him that you agree with in him, that you will no longer provide up on him, that you recognize his struggles, and that you are there for him. Far too many instructors forget about to do this -- to inform and exhibit their college students they without a doubt accept as true with in them." Among the many research-driven discussions of pedagogy and instructing strategies, it can be effortless to neglect the strength of without a doubt reassuring and encouraging your college students verbally to instill self assurance in their abilities.

Harness the strength of EdTech -- Most instructors agree instructional technological know-how is a beneficial educating tool: Using academic science in the school room makes it simpler to train college students of all mastering backgrounds, assisting instructors carry even the most timid of college students out of their shells. Curriculum-aligned math games, such as Prodigy, enhance pupil self belief and mastering outcomes. As you've in all likelihood found, college students may additionally discover math unapproachable when it's defined on the chalkboard. Grounding math in a fun, video-game surroundings that appeals to college students can produce fantastic modifications in getting to know outcomes, and even take a look at scores.

1. *Make learning goal-oriented*

- **If you set defined goals with your students** -- at the beginning of the school year or even of each lesson -- the whole class will have a better understanding of its individual and collective accomplishments. To make learning more goal-oriented, make decisive statements about the day's learning goals. For example, start a lesson with a statement such as "today you will learn the first step of multiplication," and finish the class by saying, "Congratulations! Now you're ready to show your parents you're learning how to multiply!" Cultivating this perspective helps students take confidence from their own progress, boosting learning outcomes and motivation.

- **Reassure your students verbally** -- if you want a student to believe in himself, "then actually tell him that you believe in him, that you will not give up on him, that you understand his struggles, and that you are there for them. Far too many teachers forget to do this -- to tell and show their students they actually believe in them." Among the many research-driven discussions of pedagogy and teaching strategies, it can be easy to forget the power of simply reassuring and encouraging your students verbally to instill confidence in their abilities.

2. A good teacher manages the classroom effectively

A teacher can be knowledgeable, prepared -- and even a great communicator -- but still fail simply because of an inability to deal with misbehavior in the classroom.Classroom management encompasses all the strategies a teacher deploys to organize and arrange students, learning materials, space, and use of classroom time to maximize the efficiency of teaching and learning.This helps students enjoy an organized, structured environment with an emphasis on a positive educational atmosphere that is conducive to learning.

Teacher skills for effective classroom management

- **Define Classroom Rules** -- In his book Classroom Management That Works, researcher Robert Marzano argues effective teachers "have a minimum number of classroom rules, which tend to focus on expectations of how to act toward one another, maintain a safe environment, and participate in learning." These teachers offer clear explanations of the rules, model the rules, rehearse the expectations with students, and offer the classroom "opportunities to be successful in meeting the expectations." While there is no magic number of rules that govern a classroom, it's clear the establishment of fair, reasonable, enforceable, and consistently applied rules will have a deep impact on behavior in the classroom.

- **Establish a routine** -- In a study to assess the characteristics of effective teachers, researchers found that instructors who "use classroom routines as a means of enforcing high standards for classroom behavior" enjoy greater success. To cultivate a positive and orderly learning environment, establish a routine and system wherever necessary for your daily tasks and requirements -- from the general to the specific. For example, if a student becomes stuck on an assignment, outline clear, teacher-approved guidelines for seeking help in a timely way (e.g., asking peers for assistance and -- if still unsolved -- seeking the teacher's help).
- **Consider a flexible seating arrangement** -- Research has shown that physically adjusting the classroom environment can foster greater collaboration, communication, and interaction between students and teachers alike. Flexible seating can facilitate teacher-child interaction on a level beyond what's commonly seen in traditional, teacher-fronted settings. Moreover, the novelty and stimulation students enjoy through an interactive and changing classroom setting positively impacts behavior, according to Sheryl Feinstein's book *From the Brain to the Classroom*. Flexible seating classrooms can solve a problem often seen in fixed classrooms, in which students "tend to seek out their own stimulation through movement, off-task talking, or disruptive behaviors."

3. A good teacher is prepared

Every day, the effective teacher comes to class prepared to teach.

As James Stronge writes in his influential book Qualities of Effective Teachers, "organizing time and preparing materials in advance of instruction have been noted as [among] the most important aspects of effective teaching.

"But "preparation" can be a confusing term; two different teachers might have completely different definitions of what, exactly, constitutes a truly "prepared" instructor. Consider the action items below to bolster your preparation -- and ensure you feel confident addressing your class at the start of every lesson.

Teacher skills for effective preparation

Know your content -- In chapter three of Educating Teachers of Science, Mathematics, and Technology, the authors argue that content preparation is critical for high-quality teaching, writing that it is "positively related to student achievement within specific subjects, especially in mathematics and science." So, how can you be more prepared with your content knowledge? Consider the three pillars highlighted among the INTASC Core Principles on the Expectations of Teachers' Content:

- **Knowledge** -- The teacher understands major concepts, assumptions, debates, processes of inquiry, and ways of knowing that are central to the discipline(s) s/he teaches.
- **Dispositions** -- The teacher realizes that subject matter knowledge is not a fixed body of facts but is complex and ever evolving. S/he seeks to keep abreast of new ideas and understandings in the field
- **Performances** -- The teacher effectively uses multiple representations and explanations of disciplinary

concepts that capture key ideas and link them to students' prior understandings.

Courtesy of the Yale Center for Teaching and Learning, consider the following list, "The Types of Things that Teachers Often Do to Prepare for Class":

1. Do the reading and problem sets
2. Take notes on the material
3. Review lecture notes for the week
4. Prepare an outline of issues to cover in class
5. Make a list of questions to use in class or write on the board
6. Make a handout of topics to discuss in class
7. Make a study guide to hand out
8. Design a homework assignment or question for students to prepare for a future class
9. Compile bibliographies or other outside information related to the material
10. Assemble visual material
11. Prepare supplemental reading
12. Prepare handouts on writing tips, research methods, problem solving, lab techniques, etc.
13. Meet with the professor and/or other TFs to discuss the material and how to present it in section
14. Review students' questions to anticipate their concerns, problems, interests
15. Make up quizzes
16. Devise debates, small group discussion, or other interactive projects
17. Copy articles relevant to the discussion at hand from newspapers and other periodicals

4. A good teacher sets high expectations

Effective teachers don't set limits on their students. They have high standards, they consistently challenge students to do their best, and they are caring professionals who teach students to believe in themselves.

As an educator, you know you should always expect the best of your students and encourage them to learn to their utmost potential. But you also know doing so on a daily basis can be incredibly challenging. Fortunately, there are a number of useful ways to set high expectations without burning yourself -- or your students -- out.

Teacher skills for setting high expectations

- **Don't praise low quality work** -- In the book High Expectations Teaching, researcher and educational consultant Jon Saphier declares, "Praising low quality work communicates low expectations." Communicating that message can have grave consequences. If you communicate low expectations to already underachieving students, "you are not ... pushing them to meet standards they could actually reach." While you may encourage students with good intentions, doing so when they hand in or deliver substandard work can negatively impact the learning process on a fundamental level. This highlights the importance of using praise and rewards strategically -- and emphasizes the significance of using feedback correctly as a teacher.
- **Check for understanding** -- Teachers with high expectations don't want any students going out the door

without knowing where they stand on the day's content. Check students' understanding (for example, by doing a formative assessment) as a dedicated daily (or, to start, weekly) commitment in every lesson. For example, checking questions, performing over-the-shoulder observations of student work, and listening in to group talk are all strategies you can use to communicate your high expectations as a teacher.

- **React to changes in performance** -- A dramatic downturn in a student's performance represents an opportunity to send strong messages surrounding your academic expectations. A student whose performance has dipped may be told, "This is not the standard of work I know you're capable of. We need to find out what is happening and make a plan to get you back on track." Such a remark from a respected teacher can, according to Jon Saphier, "be a powerful spur to a flagging student." Note that the language around reacting to negative behaviors -- as with writing report card comments -- requires tact and subtlety; ensure that you frame the comment in a way that provokes the student to consider their own ability to do well. Try to get your students to consider not only that they have the ability to do well, but there is something they have done to bring about the result.

- **Deliver feedback according to criteria for success** -- Research on teaching skills shows positive feedback to be a critical skill for teachers to master, with middle school teacher Hattie Marzano writing, "The most powerful single modification that enhances student achievement is feedback." Skilful feedback does not simply declare work to be right or wrong, but enables self-correction and self-adjustment. For example, instead of simply saying "You have stated the author's point of view correctly," develop your feedback, adding something such as "...but you are missing the reasons behind that point of view. Try to ... " Marzano notes a teacher's feedback is a "tacit expression of confidence ... embedded in the language used about how capable we think students are." If your feedback is actionable, frequent, detailed, and specific, students will understand you want them to succeed and are supporting them in their effort to master materials.

5. A good teacher practices self-reflection

A 2010 study about the role of critical reflection in teacher education declared teachers "must continually examine and evaluate their attitudes, practices, effectiveness, and accomplishments." The same study observed that critical reflection enhances teachers' knowledge and skills, finding it can help instructors "deeply understand the ways in which their teaching styles enhance their ability to challenge the traditional mode of practice" and to "define how they will grow as teachers."Without reflection, you run the continual risk of making poor decisions, using bad judgment, or unquestioningly believing that students can always accurately interpret your actions as intended. Without the tendency to assess your own abilities, you may continue to plan and teach on the basis of unexamined assumptions -- and remain unaware of your biggest strengths and weaknesses.

Teacher skills for self-reflection

- Use a daily reflection tool such as a journal -- In its most basic terms, the goal of journal writing is to provide a record of the significant learning experiences that have taken place during the school day. This helps you take stock of the day's events and, eventually, identify what strengths and weaknesses consistently come up -- helping you pause, review, and gain some perspective on the day's lesson(s), and, by extension, your skills as a teacher. Moreover, using a journal to record classroom anecdotes will help when it comes time to write report cards or assessments. No matter how involved you are in your students' progress, it can still be difficult to produce specific examples related to student performance if you haven't recorded them along the way.

- Try peer observation – Peer observation provides a chance for instructors to view, assess and learn from one another's teaching. This helps expose teachers to different instructional styles and strategies, stimulating critical reflection on their own classroom habits and methodologies. You might be surprised at how enjoyable the process is -- and how willing your colleagues are to collaborate!

- Record lessons -- While there are a number of potential insights you can gain from diaries and written self-assessments, they can't always capture the dynamic, day-to-day processes and events of classroom teaching. Many notable classroom events may not have been observed by the teacher -- or even remembered -- thus exemplifying the value of diaries or self-reports with audio recordings of actual lessons.

- Practice self-inquiry -- Posing "what and why" questions give teachers an important sense of perspective and power over their teaching. Researchers Ryan & Cooper developed a set of questions for reflective teachers to ask:

1. What am I doing and why?
2. How can I better meet my students' needs?
3. What options are available?
4. How can I encourage more involvement or learning on the part of the students?
5. Have I considered my own values as a professional and my comfort level acting on those values?
6. What conscious choice can I make to make a difference?

6. A good teacher uses teaching strategies

As most educators know, the traditional, teacher-focused, lecture-style teaching method can lead to disengagement and boredom (for both teachers and students) quite quickly.

That's where the deployment of different teaching strategies comes into play.

In her book Effective Teaching and Learning, Naga Subramani argues that the effective teacher "constantly renews himself [or herself] as a professional on his [or her] quest to provide students with the highest quality of education possible. This teacher has no fear of learning new teaching strategies or incorporating new technologies into lessons."

You can exhibit this spirit of "fearlessness" with a variety of fun, dynamic and engaging teaching strategies that benefit both the teacher and the student.

Should the qualities of a good teacher be defined solely by student achievement?Or should they encompass traits more difficult to measure -- such as the capacity to connect emotionally with children?Among the sea of advice, tips, and quotes on teaching, the best solution is to turn to the research.We pored through hundreds of pages of scholarship, studies, and firsthand accounts about what defines great teaching.We discovered 6 key behaviours that make a great teacher -- and defined 25 specific, actionable ways to apply those behaviours in the classroom. Start testing them with your students to stimulate a more exciting, dynamic, and engaging experience in your coming lessons!

1. A good teacher instills confidence

In the book 50 Ways to Improve Student Behavior, middle school teacher Todd Whitaker highlights low student confidence as one of the most persistent obstacles to the success of any teacher. He breaks down a worrying trend:

Many students do not believe that their teachers actually believe in them

Many students do not believe that their parents actually believe in them

Many students do not believe that any adult actually believes in them

Many students, therefore, do not believe in themselves

Students who do not believe in themselves tend to have more behavioral and academic problems

If the final point's conclusion is obvious, the inverse should be just as clear: If students who don't believe in themselves have issues in the classroom, those who do believe in themselves will be better-equipped to succeed academically.This insight is backed by a 2011 study suggesting student confidence is positively correlated with academic performance and behavioral improvement.

Teacher skills to build student confidence

Make learning goal-oriented -- If you set defined goals with your students -- at the beginning of the school year or even of each lesson -- the whole class will have a better understanding of its individual and collective accomplishments. To make learning more goal-oriented, make decisive statements about the day's learning goals. For example, start a lesson with a statement such as "today you will learn the first step of multiplication," and finish the class by saying, "Congratulations! Now you're ready to show your parents you're learning how to multiply!" Cultivating this perspective helps students take confidence from their own progress, boosting learning outcomes and motivation.

Instill a growth mindset -- According to psychologist Carol Dweck, a fixed mindset conceives of student skills as rigid and inflexible. In contrast, a growth mindset views student learning as fluid and changing, and aims to develop children's skills and talents through effort and persistence. The growth mindset, Dweck notes, helps students become more receptive to lessons and feedback. While the details of the pedagogy can be subtle, a few common ways to instill a growth mindset include actions as simple as encouraging students to expand their answers more consistently or using success folders.

Reassure your students verbally -- As elementary teacher Todd Whittaker argues, if you want a student to believe in himself, "then actually tell him that you believe in him, that you will not give up on him, that you understand his struggles, and that you are there for him. Far too many teachers forget to do this -- to tell and show their students they actually believe in them." Among the many research-driven discussions of pedagogy and teaching strategies, it can be easy to forget the power of simply reassuring and encouraging your students verbally to instill confidence in their abilities.

Harness the power of EdTech -- Most teachers agree educational technology is a useful teaching tool: In a study conducted by the Joan Ganz Cooney Center, almost 80% of K-8 classroom teachers surveyed said that digital games have "improved student mastery of curricular content". Using educational technology in the classroom makes it easier to teach students of all learning backgrounds, helping teachers bring even the most timid of students out of their shells. Curriculum-aligned math games, such as Prodigy, boost student confidence and learning outcomes. As you've likely found, students may find math unapproachable when it's explained on the chalkboard. Grounding math in a fun, video-game environment that appeals to students can produce remarkable changes in learning outcomes, and even test scores.

2. A good teacher manages the classroom effectively

A teacher can be knowledgeable, prepared -- and even a great communicator -- but still fail simply because of an inability to deal with misbehavior in the classroom.Classroom management encompasses all the strategies a teacher deploys to organize and arrange students, learning materials, space, and use of classroom time to maximize the efficiency of teaching and learning.This helps students enjoy an organized, structured environment with an emphasis on a positive educational atmosphere that is conducive to learning.Teacher skills for effective classroom management

Define Classroom Rules -- In his book Classroom Management That Works, researcher Robert Marzano argues effective teachers "have a minimum number of classroom rules, which tend to focus on expectations of how to act toward one another, maintain a safe environment, and participate in learning." These teachers offer clear explanations of the rules, model the rules, rehearse the expectations with students, and offer the classroom "opportunities to be successful in meeting the expectations." While there is no magic number of rules that govern a classroom, it's clear the establishment of fair, reasonable, enforceable, and consistently applied rules will have a deep impact on behavior in the classroom.

Establish a routine -- In a study to assess the characteristics of effective teachers, researchers found that instructors who "use classroom routines as a means of enforcing high standards for classroom behavior" enjoy greater success. To cultivate a positive and orderly learning environment, establish a routine and system wherever necessary for your daily tasks and requirements -- from the general to the specific. For example, if a student becomes stuck on an assignment, outline clear, teacher-approved guidelines for seeking help in a timely way (e.g., asking peers for assistance and -- if still unsolved -- seeking the teacher's help).

Consider a flexible seating arrangement -- Research has shown that physically adjusting the classroom environment can foster greater collaboration, communication, and interaction between students and teachers alike. Flexible seating can facilitate teacher-child interaction on a level beyond what's commonly seen in traditional, teacher-fronted settings. Moreover, the novelty and stimulation students enjoy through an interactive and changing classroom setting positively impacts behavior, according to Sheryl Feinstein's book From the Brain to the Classroom. Flexible seating classrooms can solve a problem often seen in fixed classrooms, in which students "tend to seek out their own stimulation through movement, off-task talking, or disruptive behaviors."

3. A good teacher is prepared

Every day, the effective teacher comes to class prepared to teach. As James Stronge writes in his influential book Qualities of Effective Teachers, "organizing time and preparing materials in advance of instruction have been noted as [among] the most important aspects of effective teaching."But "preparation" can be a confusing term; two different teachers might have completely different definitions of what, exactly, constitutes a truly "prepared" instructor. Consider the action items below to bolster your preparation -- and ensure you feel confident addressing your class at the start of every lesson.

Teacher skills for effective preparation

Know your content -- In chapter three of Educating Teachers of Science, Mathematics, and Technology, the authors argue that content preparation is critical for high-quality teaching, writing that it is "positively related to student achievement within specific subjects, especially in mathematics and science." So, how can you be more prepared with your content knowledge? Consider the three pillars highlighted among the INTASC Core Principles on the Expectations of Teachers' Content:

Knowledge -- The teacher understands major concepts, assumptions, debates, processes of inquiry, and ways of knowing that are central to the discipline(s) s/he teaches.

Dispositions -- The teacher realizes that subject matter knowledge is not a fixed body of facts but is complex and ever evolving. S/he seeks to keep abreast of new ideas and understandings in the field

Performances -- The teacher effectively uses multiple representations and explanations of disciplinary concepts that capture key ideas and link them to students' prior understandings.

Courtesy of the Yale Center for Teaching and Learning, consider the following list, "The Types of Things that Teachers Often Do to Prepare for Class":

Do the reading and problem sets

Take notes on the material

Review lecture notes for the week

Prepare an outline of issues to cover in class

Make a list of questions to use in class or write on the board

Make a handout of topics to discuss in class

Make a study guide to hand out

Design a homework assignment or question for students to prepare for a future class

Compile bibliographies or other outside information related to the material

Assemble visual material

Prepare supplemental reading

Prepare handouts on writing tips, research methods, problem solving, lab techniques, etc.

Meet with the professor and/or other TFs to discuss the material and how to present it in section

Review students' questions to anticipate their concerns, problems, interests

Make up quizzes

Devise debates, small group discussion, or other interactive projects

Copy articles relevant to the discussion at hand from newspapers and other periodicals

4. A good teacher sets high expectations

Effective teachers don't set limits on their students. They have high standards, they consistently challenge students to do their best, and they are caring professionals who teach students to believe in themselves.As an educator, you know you should always expect the best of your students and encourage them to learn to their utmost potential. But you also know doing so on a daily basis can be incredibly challenging. Fortunately, there are a number of useful ways to set high expectations without burning yourself -- or your students -- out.

Teacher skills for setting high expectations

Don't praise low quality work -- In the book High Expectations Teaching, researcher and educational consultant Jon Saphier declares, "Praising low quality work communicates low expectations." Communicating that message can have grave consequences. If you communicate low expectations to already underachieving students, "you are not ... pushing them to meet standards they could actually reach." While you may encourage students with good intentions, doing so when they hand in or deliver substandard work can negatively impact the learning process on a fundamental level. This highlights the importance of using praise and rewards strategically -- and emphasizes the significance of using feedback correctly as a teacher.

Check for understanding -- Teachers with high expectations don't want any students going out the door without knowing where they stand on the day's content.

Check students' understanding (for example, by doing a formative assessment) as a dedicated daily (or, to start, weekly) commitment in every lesson. For example, checking questions, performing over-the-shoulder observations of student work, and listening in to group talk are all strategies you can use to communicate your high expectations as a teacher.

React to changes in performance -- A dramatic downturn in a student's performance represents an opportunity to send strong messages surrounding your academic expectations. A student whose performance has dipped may be told, "This is not the standard of work I know you're capable of. We need to find out what is happening and make a plan to get you back on track." Such a remark from a respected teacher can, according to Jon Saphier, "be a powerful spur to a flagging student." Note that the language around reacting to negative behaviors -- as with writing report card comments -- requires tact and subtlety; ensure that you frame the comment in a way that provokes the student to consider their own ability to do well. Try to get your students to consider not only that they have the ability to do well, but there is something they have done to bring about the result.

Deliver feedback according to criteria for success -- Research on teaching skills shows positive feedback to be a critical skill for teachers to master, with middle school teacher Hattie Marzano writing, "The most powerful single modification that enhances student achievement is feedback." Skilful feedback does not simply declare work to be right or wrong, but enables self-correction and self-adjustment. For example, instead of simply saying "You have stated the author's point of view correctly," develop your feedback, adding something such as "...but you are missing the reasons behind that point of view. Try to ... " Marzano notes a teacher's feedback is a "tacit expression of confidence ... embedded in the language used about how capable we think students are." If your feedback is actionable, frequent, detailed, and specific, students will understand you want them to succeed and are supporting them in their effort to master materials.

5. A good teacher practices self-reflection

A 2010 study about the role of critical reflection in teacher education declared teachers "must continually examine and evaluate their attitudes, practices, effectiveness, and accomplishments." The same study observed that critical reflection enhances teachers' knowledge and skills, finding it can help instructors "deeply understand the ways in which their teaching styles enhance their ability to challenge the traditional mode of practice" and to "define how they will grow as teachers."Without reflection, you run the continual risk of making poor decisions, using bad judgment, or unquestioningly believing that students can always accurately interpret your actions as intended. Without the tendency to assess your own abilities, you may continue to plan and teach on the basis of unexamined assumptions -- and remain unaware of your biggest strengths and weaknesses.

Teacher skills for self-reflection

Use a daily reflection tool such as a journal -- In its most basic terms, the goal of journal writing is to provide a record of the significant learning experiences that have taken place during the school day. This helps you take stock of the day's events and, eventually, identify what strengths and weaknesses consistently come up -- helping you pause, review, and gain some perspective on the day's lesson(s), and, by extension, your skills as a teacher. Moreover, using a journal to record classroom anecdotes will help when it comes time to write report cards or assessments. No matter how involved you are in your students' progress, it can still be difficult to produce specific examples related to student performance if you haven't recorded them along the way.

Try peer observation – Peer observation provides a chance for instructors to view, assess and learn from one another's teaching. This helps expose teachers to different instructional styles and strategies, stimulating critical reflection on their own classroom habits and methodologies. You might be surprised at how enjoyable the process is -- and how willing your colleagues are to collaborate!

Record lessons -- While there are a number of potential insights you can gain from diaries and written self-assessments, they can't always capture the dynamic, day-to-day processes and events of classroom teaching. Many notable classroom events may not have been observed by the teacher -- or even remembered -- thus exemplifying the value of diaries or self-reports with audio recordings of actual lessons.

Practice self-inquiry -- Posing "what and why" questions give teachers an important sense of perspective and power over their teaching. Researchers Ryan & Cooper developed a set of questions for reflective teachers to ask:

What am I doing and why?

How can I better meet my students' needs?

What options are available?

How can I encourage more involvement or learning on the part of the students?

Have I considered my own values as a professional and my comfort level acting on those values?

What conscious choice can I make to make a difference?

A self-assessment: What are the qualities of a good teacher?

Based on the research of Jeffrey Glanz in his book Classroom Strategies for the Beginning Teacher, there are eight categories to consider when quizzing your own teaching skills:

Teacher Skills Category

Question

Content (subject and general knowledge)Do you have a strong grasp of the content you are teaching?

PedagogicalAre you well-versed and confident with teaching theory, learning theory, and curriculum theory?

SelfDo you know yourself well (e.g. your strengths, limitations, etc.)?

Interpersonal (students, parents, administration, community)Do you relate well to others? How do you know?

QuestioningDo you pose varied, thought-provoking questions?

PlanningDo you always plan for instruction? Consequences of poor planning include behavior problems, lack of learning, monotonous presentation, lack of respect for teacher, etc.)

Classroom ManagementAre you having difficulty with classroom management and implementing an effective disciplinary plan?

CommunicationAre you a good communicator? How do you know?

6. A good teacher uses teaching strategies

As most educators know, the traditional, teacher-focused, lecture-style teaching method can lead to disengagement and boredom (for both teachers and students) quite quickly.That's where the deployment of different teaching strategies comes into play.In her book Effective Teaching and Learning, Naga Subramani argues that the effective teacher "constantly renews himself [or herself] as a professional on his [or her] quest to provide students with the highest quality of education possible. This teacher has no fear of learning new teaching strategies or incorporating new technologies into lessons."You can exhibit this spirit of "fearlessness" with a variety of fun, dynamic and engaging teaching strategies that benefit both the teacher and the student.

Some of the more prominent and useful teaching strategies are outlined below:

- Active learning strategies put students at the center of the learning process, enriching the classroom experience and boosting engagement. Use them to help students talk more openly, think more creatively and — ultimately — feel more engaged in the process of learning.
- Experiential learning activities build knowledge and skills through direct experience, deploying a student-centered approach that empowers participants to take learning into their own hands and apply it in an engaging context.
- Project-based learning uses an open-ended approach in which students work alone or collectively to produce an engaging, intricate curriculum-related questions or challenges. Encourage students to apply skills and knowledge they've developed in your classes, and allow students to take their own approaches to develop an answer and deliver a product.

- Inquiry-based learning is a learning and teaching method that prioritizes student questions, ideas and analyses. It is subdivided into four categories, all of which promote the importance of students' role in the development of thought-provoking questions and ideas.
- Adaptive learning focuses on changing — or "adapting" — learning content for students on an individual basis, particularly with the help of technology.
- Cooperative learning involves delivering instruction through small groups, empowering students to work together to build their understanding of a variety of topics and concepts.
- Differentiated instruction is most aptly defined by its responsiveness to students' learning preferences, and involves the ongoing use of assessment to collect information about where students are in their learning. Teachers apply this information to vary the learning environment, instruction, and assessment and evaluation.

The Qualities of a Good Teacher: Final Thoughts

There is no single solution to the question of what makes a great teacher.

To those who have never taught, it is difficult to grasp how diverse and dynamic a skillset one needs to succeed in a busy, demanding classroom setting.

For some, these challenges are overwhelming.But they don't have to be.Consider these six qualities -- and the actionable methods for putting them into practice -- to sharpen and develop your own skills. The results, as you may find, can make all the difference.

CHAPTER FOUR

BAD TEACHER

One would hope that all teachers would strive to be excellent, effective educators. However, education is just like any other profession. There are those who work extremely hard at their craft getting better on a daily basis and there are those that are just simply there never striving to improve. Even though this type of teacher is in the minority, just a handful of truly bad teachers can hurt the profession.

Their is nothing bad about teachers but in my opinion some of the teachers didn't pay attention towards weak students they only deal with intelligent ones in the class due to this weaker ones feels shy to share their problems they get weaker and weaker day by day on the other hand they are not treated equivalent in the classroom by teachers as well as other students too

1. Ego. A teacher who can't let go of some grand idea of his own greatness can never impart his knowledge to his pupil.
2. Lack of empathy. Students come from different backgrounds, everyone with different capabilities. If a teacher cannot at least try and get to know what are

the difficulties they are facing, hopelessness engulfs the students very quickly.

3. Impatience and Dismissive nature. "Don't ask these kind of stupid questions" is one of the phrases which every student might have heard at least once. This kind of attitude discourages students from ever asking a question and it gradually kills his enthusiasm for knowledge.

4. Lack of motivation. If you don't have interest in teaching, just don't. Doing a half assed job doesn't help anyone. Not even you.

5. Reading straight out of the book. I have experienced such as teacher in my school life they just read the line of text book, and nothing to explan about it and waiting for other student to let them read for everyone. Reading is fine art but with the reading, the teacher should explain those line which the teacher had reads

6. They dictate too fast. *We are kids, not stenographers :- by one of my Student*

7. A bad teacher insults child in front of other children. Comparing a child with other children. These things would discourage a child.

8. Punishing the student by making him / her stand outside of the class

- I go to a private Christian school, and I must say I've been blessed to have mostly wonderful teachers. That said, I have had a few bad teachers, mostly substitutes. Here are a few qualities that turn students off from teachers:

- Lying. I think this kind of goes without saying, but don't lie to your students, especially if you're a substitute teacher. Last year my Bible teacher missed a few weeks of school to have back surgery, and the day after he had it, our sub (whom everyone hates) told his hometown class that he'd died. Needless to say, we were all pretty shocked, horrified, and pissed off.

- Not keeping your promises. If you say you'll have our tests graded by Thursday, we're going to expect our tests to be graded by Thursday. We understand that you have other classes too, but don't promise something you'll wind up not fulfilling.

- Insulting a student. Especially their grades. One time a student got an A on a test only to have the teacher deliver this backhanded insult: "Good job! I didn't think you could do it." That's rude, disrespectful, and unacceptable. Don't do it.

Not willing to accept mistakes

Student: "Excuse me but you got question 13 wrong. Its supposed to be-"

Teacher: "No I am right. The textbook said so."

Student: "Yes, but-"

Teacher: "Are you trying to argue with me?!"

Plays favourites

Teacher: " I am giving you detention for talking in class."

Student A: "What?! But Student B was also talking!"

Teacher: "That's none of my concern."

Can only follow the textbook

Teacher: "(Reads from the textbook)"

Student: "I don't understand. Can you explain it?"

Teacher: "(Reads from the textbook again)"

What defines a bad teacher

1. A teacher who regurgitates information from a PowerPoint presentation.
2. A teacher who presents to you a message bunch of facts, but knows nothing about those facts.
3. The teachers who ignore you.
4. The teachers who are too busy to help you.
5. A teacher who gives you a test without any notice. This used to put me in panic mode.
6. A teacher who takes forever to grade your paper.
7. A teacher who gives you rubbish feedback on your work.
8. A teacher who sits in the corner of the room and asks you to open 'page 384' of the textbook and simply sit in silence and read.
9. A teacher who doesn't engage with the students.
10. Strict teachers who think being harsh will discipline children.
11. Teachers who do nothing about students being bullied.
12. Teachers who pick on you to give the answer when you truly don't know. It's embarrassing.
13. Teachers who mock you when you give the wrong answer. This does nothing but affect the child's self esteem.
14. Teachers who hit students. This happens frequently in many parts of the world.

Moments to moments

The moment I think of what she did to me, I feel cheated and angry at the same time.

This is something that I can never forget in my entire life.

I was in 11th class.

Half-yearly exams were over and it was time to review our answer sheets.

I was among top 4 students of my class and a single difference in mark could make a change in the rankings.

Our respected teacher distributed the *subject* answer sheets.

I got 82.7 marks.

Not bad.

My classmate got 83.4 which was the highest.

But wait!

On calculating the total again, I realized that I am the topper with 88.7 marks.

I was overjoyed and started jumping because being the topper was one of the best feelings for any student.

Excuse me Mam!

"The total is coming out to be 88.7, you missed 6 marks here" I told her politely.

"Let me check"

She first calculated the total and it was again 88.7.

Then she started searching my entire answer sheet and pointing out to an answer said "Ye answer toh ghalat hai" (This answer is wrong)

"But I wrote this from your notes mam"

"Pata nahi kaise maine tick kar diya isko, ghalat hai" she said while crossing that answer and deducting 2 marks and again 2 marks and again 2 marks.

(Don't know how I gave you marks on this one, it's a wrong answer)

"Count the total now, see it's 82.7 only" she said while giving a villain kinda smile.

It did not take much time for me to understand her intention.

Her favorite student, who scored 83.4, was not becoming the topper because of me.

She, being the teacher, used her "power" and dragged me back to the second position.

All I could do was sit in a corner and wonder how could a teacher play so unfair??

This incident might look very normal now but if you try to think it from a student's perspective who worked hard but was not given the fair share, you might be able to feel the pain and disappointment that I felt that day.

Teachers are meant to be impartial, fair and honest. Afteral, they are examples for us, live examples.

We all are novice in school and hence, the role of teacher becomes more crucial because they have a great impact on our personality and thinking.

Please act fair in your life!

Traits of a Bad Teacher

Lack of Classroom Management
A lack of classroom management is probably the single biggest downfall of a bad teacher. This issue can be the demise of any teacher no matter their intentions. If a teacher cannot control their students, they will not be able to teach them effectively. Being a good classroom manager starts on day one by incorporating simple procedures and expectations and then following through on predetermined consequences when those procedures and expectations are compromised.

Lack of Content Knowledge

Most states require teachers to pass a comprehensive series of assessments to obtain certification within a specific subject area. With this requirement, you would think that all teachers would be proficient enough to teach the subject area(s) they were hired to teach. Unfortunately, there are some teachers who do not know the content well enough to teach it. This is an area that could be overcome through preparation. All teachers should thoroughly prepare for any lesson before they teach it to make sure they understand what they are going to be teaching. Teachers will lose credibility with their students quickly if they do not know what they are teaching, thus making them ineffective.

Lack of Organizational Skills

Effective teachers must be organized. Teachers who lack organizational skills will be overwhelmed and, as a result, ineffective. Teachers who recognize a weakness in organization should seek help in improving in that area. Organizational skills can be improved with some good direction and advice.

Lack of Professionalism

Professionalism encompasses many different areas of teaching. A lack of professionalism can quickly result in a teacher's dismissal. Ineffective teachers are often tardy or absent. They may fail to follow a district's dress code or use inappropriate language in their classroom.

Poor Judgment

Too many good teachers have lost their careers due to a moment of poor judgment. Common sense goes a long way in protecting yourself from these sorts of scenarios. A good teacher will think before acting, even in moments where emotions or stressors are running high.

Poor People Skills

Good communication is essential in the teaching profession. An ineffective teacher communicates poorly, or not at all, with students, parents, other teachers, staff members, and administrators. They leave parents out of the loop about what is happening in the classroom.

Lack of Commitment

There are some teachers who simply lack motivation. They spend the minimum amount of time necessary to do their job never arriving early or staying late. They do not challenge their students, are often behind on grading, show videos often, and give "free" days on a regular basis. There is no creativity in their teaching, and they typically make no connections with other faculty or staff members.

There is no such thing as a perfect teacher. It is in the nature of the profession to continuously improve in all areas, including classroom management, teaching style, communication, and subject area knowledge. What matters most is a commitment to improvement. If a teacher lacks this commitment, they may not be suited for the profession. *Meador, Derrick. "Traits of a Bad Teacher." ThoughtCo, Aug. 26, 2020,*

CHAPTER FIVE

TEACHERS CAN BE ROLE MODELS

There are many reasons why students think of teachers as role models. One of the biggest reasons is the desire to become a role model for students to look up to, to learn from, and to remember for the rest of their lives. Everyone has felt the power and lasting presence of an effective teacher, who also had a bigger impact. Whether it's learning the value of community service, discovering a love for a particular subject, or how to tap the confidence to speak in public, teachers are the ones who light the way for us in this world.

Teachers being role models is not a new concept, and has inspired students to go into this field for ages. If you are thinking about becoming a teacher, good for you! We are here to root you on and help you make the right decision. Your next step would be speaking with schools in your area. Luckily, we have relationships with schools in every state with education programs. Just use the simple search function at the top of this page, or browse the listings below.

Here are some ways of the importance of teachers

1.) Be humble. There is nothing that teaches a child or young adult mature behavior like modeling it yourself. This isn't just true when you are right. You also have to show your students what it is like to be wrong, and admit it. This is never easy, no matter how old you are. Especially when you are in front of several students who look up to you. And let's face it, there are some students who aren't going to feel sorry for you. But that's life. And you have to show them that right is right, and wrong is wrong – no matter what.

2.) Encourage them to think for themselves. Treat your classroom like a group of individuals, and celebrate their diversity. Create activities and discussions that foster conversations and discovery about who they are, and how they can appreciate the differences between each other. This type of focus from time-to-time will build a stronger bond between your students. Also, an environment of trust will build, which can relax the atmosphere and help students focus more on learning. It's also important to help students understand the way they learn, and encourage them to explore those parts of themselves as well.

3.) Perform volunteer work. Find a way to incorporate community service into one of your lessons, and discuss how you contribute to the community you live in. Ask your students to tell you ways you could perform community service as a group. Many schools will give students a certain amount of time off if they are doing an activity that falls into this category. See if you can organize a community service event with your class. For example, if you are a music teacher, you can take your class caroling at a retirement home. Or, you can have your class pick up litter on a stretch of road. There are many ways you can instill a sense of pride in giving back among your students.

4.) Show empathy. When we think of teachers as role models, we imagine sympathetic mentors who listen to their students. Sounds simple, right? All you have to do is show that you care? It may sound simple, but we have all had teachers that we didn't connect with. Students can tell when a teacher is tuned in or tuned out, and disconnected from them. On the opposite end of the spectrum, we have all had teachers who went out of their way to show they care about us, and want to see us succeed. We all have different personalities, and you should be authentic. But be mindful that your students are looking up to you as an adult with life experience they don't have. As they try to figure out how to move into adulthood, make sure they know you've got their back.

5.) Point out the positive. Create a culture in your classroom that rewards kind behavior. The importance of teachers is apparent in the link between positive reinforcement and their confidence and behavior. Teach them to be constructive with their criticism, pointing out positives before negative, or suggestions for improvement. Practice with exercises that allows the students to be positive and critical towards each other. This is the kind of respect that debate class exercises can teach children – how to agree to disagree. Teaching children to get in the habit of looking for good in others is never a bad role model for behavior.

6.) Celebrate the arts. Teachers being role models by helping students appreciate the arts isn't the first thing that comes to people's minds. But helping children connect with their own inner children by tapping into the arts. Even if you do not teach a creative subject, you can incorporate music, discussions about art, and give students artistic assignments that reflect the curriculum they are learning. Mixing it up every once in a while will keep their minds fresh, and encourage them to look at life a little differently. Many students are obsessed with music, art, literature and other forms of creative expression. Give bonus points for students who pursue an independent art project that goes along with a teaching.

7.) Send a positive note home to their parents twice a year. Showing your students that you appreciate them in a direct way is important. But indirect forms of gratitude can be a boost to their confidence, and model positive behavior. Most parents never expect to get a note in their kid's bag saying what a pleasure they are to have in class. So why not give your kids a boost and let mom and dad know you care? Every parent knows, we just want our kids to do well and succeed, no matter where they are in life. This will help your relations with them as well. And we have a feeling your students will appreciate any effort you make to let their parents know they're doing alright.

8.) Fulfill your promises. Hey, remember last fall when you said you would buy the class a turtle if they earned all those stars? Well, it's been six months since they earned em and school is almost over... Okay, don't be that teacher. We're all busy. Even your students. That's why you need to follow through on your promises when you make them. We don't want to them to think it's okay to say one thing, and then completely disregard it. And if you fail to keep a particular promise, be honest about it. Don't make up an excuse. And try to make up for it. Your students will see how to deal with their own shortcomings, and will respect you more for your honesty.

9.) Dress appropriately. Look, we know how young and hip you still are. No one wants to be uncool. But teachers being role models means remembering you are in a professional environment. And it's not your job to fit in with the cool kids. It's your job to stand at the head of the class and foster a sense of mutual respect. After all, you want to model professional behavior for your students from day one. This will help with classroom management issues. Dressing in a professional way will keep students from thinking of you in a less respectful way. This goes for cleanliness and hygiene as well. Just make sure you take your job seriously when you show up. This is not only good to model for your students, but important in the eyes of your principal and other administrators as well.

10.) Stay away from social media with students. Educators as role models on social media is a new and important topic. Do not mix on social media with your students. And be careful what you have out there on your personal accounts. We are all too familiar with the stories of teachers and other professionals doing something unprofessional and getting fired for it. Have a policy to connect with students on the channels that your school sets up for you. Remember, parents are looking at you as well, and know that you are in a role model position with their children. When you post on social media, just realize that your students' parents could see your words as well. Just be careful.

11.) Encourage physical activity. The importance of teachers extends to the physical fitness of their students. It doesn't matter if every student is inclined to be physically active. Encouraging physical activity is good for all groups of students. Even if you do not teach a physical education class, you can still talk about physical activities when you lecturing or performing other activities. Even weaving the topic into your lectures or conversations can help plant the seeds in students' minds that they should look for ways to exercise.

12.) Give lectures about role models. When you are discussing a period in history, or introducing a new subject to your students, find a way to incorporate a hero story into the lesson. For instance, if you are going to talk about French history and the Hundred Years War, you would talk about the bravery of Joan of Arc. Or you could find stories about other unlikely heroes, and those who shaped history. When you do, have your students discuss ways they can be heroes in their own lives. Even if it's just stepping up in small ways to help others or do things they didn't think possible.

13.) Have them read Profiles in Courage. When we think of teachers as role models, we think of the classic novels and literature they shared with us. John F. Kennedy's Nobel Prize winning book chronicles the acts of courage by several figures throughout American history. These characters were brave enough to make tough choices in hard times, putting their country before themselves, and their personal safety. Other books can be great options, such as To Kill A Mockingbird or movies like Good Will Hunting, when you want to give your kids a break, and teach them a lesson in doing the right thing. Being a good role model for kids means showing them how to point their moral compass in the right direction no matter what. The importance of teachers cannot be overstated when it comes to reading.

14.) Hold a fundraiser. Pick a local charity and tell your students you have a goal to raise a certain amount of money within a certain period of time. You will all make a game of raising the most money and giving it to a charity. It can even be a non-organized charity. Let's say you hear about someone in your community who lost their home to a fire. You could raise the money and give them a gift card or something they may need. There are all sorts of ways you can incorporate the idea of fundraising and charity. Be sure to include all your students in the process somehow. These types of exercises can also help give them leadership and business skills.

15.) Discuss world events. Every Monday, or on some kind of schedule, spark discussions about world events. See what they know, and ask questions that make them think. Teachers being role models includes showing students how to make sense of the world, and express different ideas in a peaceful way. This can model for students how they should act when they speak with others, and how to actively listen to other points of view. Many students will not have heard about some of the events you are speaking about. Don't let them sit back quietly. Find ways to involve them too, by asking questions that can draw them in.

16.) Have a pot luck. Every once in a while, have a meal with your students that celebrates you time together. Yes, food is another way students can see educators as role models. So have fun with this one. After all, we all love food! Tell your students that they are welcome to bring a dish from home, or you can provide a cheap set of snacks. This can be a good way to talk about cooking with your students. Many kids aren't involved in with the cooking at their homes. Some parents teach their kids about food, but it's probably the exception, not the norm. So, be that teacher that shows them that they can learn to cook and eat healthy foods. You can show them that good food can also be good for you!

17.) Work extracurricular activities. When your students see you working outside of the classroom to help your school function, it says you go the extra mile. It also shows that you have a strong work ethic, and you are doing a job that you're passionate about. That is the kind of feeling you want your students to have from their careers later in life. Show them that you enjoy your job, and it will pay off in the classroom. And, if you were once a star athlete and have coaching skills, you can be a role model for the students playing sports in a similar way.

18.) Be organized and on time. You want to present yourself in a professional way as much as possible. This means more than looking the part and acting the part, it means being the part. The best way you can show your students how to execute their work is to show up on time and be ready to teach. Plus, if you have a clear vision for how you want the lesson to go, then you will be more effective in delivering your message.

19.) Practice random acts of kindness. Here's an idea for teachers as role models: How about you put an apple on every one of your students' desks on the first day of school? How would that be for a proactive show of appreciation from the get-go with your class. That would also put them on notice that you are the type of teacher who will surprise them from time to time. This teaches children to go out of their way to show appreciate – even if it's just for the heck of it.

20.) Ask for input. You know that suggestion box that companies sometimes have for employees to make recommendations? These can be ideas for lectures, field trips, and other things the students think may add to the learning environment. The importance of teachers in showing students how to participate in conversations is essential to their growth. Giving them a feeling of ownership and participation in the class decisions and idea generating process will give them a sense of pride they may not have otherwise; especially if you agree to test their idea out.

21.) Apply democratic ideals to class discussions. Just because your students may not be old enough to vote, doesn't mean they can't get a feel for our democratic processes. Teachers being role models to show how our democracy works can be a great lesson for students. Hold votes on decisions that reflect discussions you are having on topics to see where people stand. Then encourage debate and explain to them how our system is supposed to work. No matter where your students might fall on the political spectrum, you can set a good example by engaging them with our core values.

22.) Invite guest lecturers. Find role models in the community that do good work, or perform some kind of public service. This can be small business owners, individuals, city officials, and other notable figures who can inspire the children to do good in their lives. Plus, it's always fun for students to learn from other people than just their own teacher. Kids need lots of role models in their lives. Plus, whoever you invite will get to share a personal story from their life, or show them how they work in their profession. There are just too many reasons why this can be a great idea!

23.) Make them keep journals. You can inspire your students to understand that it helps to keep track of your thoughts as a way of organizing your goals, connecting with your feelings, and making sense of the world around you. Your students will improve on their own communication skills through their writing practice, and have a safe space to explore their thoughts, during an otherwise hectic daily routine. When you teach students to understand themselves a little better, they will start to see educators as role models.

24.) Start a class garden. Many schools have room for classes to start their own small garden. If not, check with your county office to see if there is any land available where you can make a community garden. This can teach students about growing food, and how people have to work together to sustain our standards of living.

25.) Make them give a presentation on one of their role models. Lastly, have your students think about what makes a good role model, and present their findings to the class. It can be a famous example, or anyone who inspires your student to present. Try not to create too many rules for your students to abide by. See where their minds go, and what qualities they associate with the term

CHAPTER SIX

SUCCESSFUL

There are about a million different approaches to teaching. In general, no two teachers are alike.

Each has their own teaching style and routine. But while there is no blueprint for teaching, there is a certain code that teachers must live by if they want to be successful.

Act in your students' best interest

Always do what you believe is best for your students because as are your number one priority. Whenever making a decision, ask yourself, "How does this benefit my students?" If you can't come up with an answer, reconsider your choice.

Build important relationships

Focus on establishing meaningful, cooperative relationships with everyone you encounter. Building strong relationships with your students, peers, administrators, and parents will ultimately make your job easier.

Be explicit about rules and expectations

Clearly establish rules, expectations, and procedures on the first day of school, then discuss and reference them often. Students cannot be expected to be held accountable for their actions if they do not know how they should behave. Be firm, fair, and consistent for a classroom that runs more smoothly.

Be fair and consistent

Your students watch for this and are quick to notice disparities. Do not undermine your own authority and the relationships you have worked hard to build by playing favorites or showing prejudice.

Be prepared

Take a cue from the boy scouts and always be prepared! Preparation will not guarantee success but lack of preparation makes it much less likely. Put in the time to engage your students, craft effectual lessons, and provide useful feedback.

Learn every day

Teaching is a journey that will provide you with many opportunities to learn but you have to be open and willing to take them. You should strive to improve your teaching each and every day, even when you've been in the classroom for years.

Leave your problems at the door

Never bring your personal problems or issues into the classroom—leave them at home. Your students should never know when something in your personal life is bothering you.

Involve families

Parents can make or break their children's education, and as such, teachers must do their part to engage even the most reluctant parents in the learning process. Provide plenty of opportunities for parents and guardians to become involved and feel welcomed into your classroom.

Protect your students

Protect your students at all costs. It is your job to ensure that your students are safe and secure at all times. Practice safety procedures frequently in class and never allow students to engage in reckless behavior. Discuss safe behavior outside of school too.

Protect yourself

A teacher must never put themselves in a compromising situation that will bring harm to their career or person. They should always be aware of their surroundings and never allow themselves to be too vulnerable or have their reputation called into question. Protect yourself from danger by maintaining self-control and staying alert at all times.

Get along with administration

Respect the decisions of administrators and understand that they have many responsibilities. Teachers that have great working relationships with their administrators enjoy a more relaxed and supportive work environment.

Get to know your students

Take the time to find out what your students like to do and incorporate their interests into your lessons. Establish a rapport and connection with them not only to engage them in class but also to show that you care about them beyond their performance in school.

Listen

Always be willing to listen to others, especially your students. Use their feedback to improve your practice. Responsive teachers take the time to learn from what others have to say because they know that they are not perfect.

Assume responsibility for mistakes

Own your faults and correct your mistakes—teachers are not expected to know everything. Set a positive example for your students by calling attention to your errors and showing them that mistakes help you learn.

Seek advice from other teachers

Fellow teachers can be one of your greatest resources. Take advantage of the experiences that others have had by working cooperatively, sharing stories and materials whenever you can. You are not alone!

Be flexible

Be willing to adapt and change. There is always going to be something new to try and things to improve. Some of the best moments in teaching are born out of spontaneity—embrace change rather than resist it.

Be encouraging

Be your students' biggest cheerleader. Never tell them that they cannot do anything. Help them accomplish their goals by familiarizing yourself with their specific needs and setting them on the path to success, nudging them gently back in the right direction if they need it.

Never embarrass your students

Never put down a student, especially not in front of their peers. If you need to discipline or correct a student, do so privately and thoughtfully. Your goal is to teach and guide them when they slip up, not make them feel guilty or bad.

Have fun

Have fun! Enjoy your work and your students will take notice and follow suit. Teaching can be messy but it is better to embrace the chaos than take it too seriously.

Be involved in the lives of your students

Go the extra mile when you can. The best teachers go out of their way to attend student events such as sports and concerts to show their support. These small actions mean a lot to your students.

Provide meaningful and frequent feedback

Try not to fall behind in grading and recording and don't take shortcuts. When this task feels overwhelming, remind yourself that timely constructive feedback is worth the effort in the long run because students learn most when you check in with them about their performance.

Stay up-to-date

Always be aware of and adhere to local policies and procedures. If you are not sure about something, it is better to ask than make assumptions and mistakes. You must know and follow the rules of teaching just as you expect your students to know and follow yours.

Decompress after school

Find time to decompress outside of school. Every teacher needs to have hobbies and interests that allow them to distance themselves from the stress of school. Teaching may take up a large portion of your life but should not be all that you do. *Meador, Derrick. "24 Simple Rules All Teachers Should Live By."*

CHAPTER SEVEN

Ask Yourself to Design Your Educational Philosophy

While going through their own education, teachers are tasked with developing an educational philosophy, which is a teacher's personal statement detailing their guiding principles about such education-related issues as how students learn best, as well as the role of educators in the classroom, school, community, and society.

Why did you become a teacher?

Creating a personal philosophy of education can help you articulate your approach to teaching in a clear, concise way. It can also help you express why you think being a teacher is so important.

Whether you're deciding on a course of action in your classroom or answering interview questions, an educational philosophy can help you make sure you're sticking close to what matters most to you.

Contents
What is a philosophy of education?
Basic examples of educational philosophies
Questions to ask within your own philosophy
Prodigy's philosophy of education
How to constantly refine your learning process
Why did you become a teacher?

Whether it's in a job interview or a dinner with friends, chances are you've been asked some version of that question. But it's not always an easy question to answer!

Creating a personal philosophy of education can help you articulate your approach to teaching in a clear, concise way. It can also help you express why you think being a teacher is so important.

Whether you're deciding on a course of action in your classroom or answering interview questions, an educational philosophy can help you make sure you're sticking close to what matters most to you.

What is a philosophy of education?

A philosophy of education is **a set of beliefs and guiding principles for teachers.**

It helps you make decisions about how you teach your students.

It's also a useful tool when it comes time to communicate your beliefs to other people, including:

- Parents
- Your teaching team
- School administrators
- Potential employers in a job interview

Creating a philosophy of education is a great way to set teaching goals for yourself, and can even help you identify areas for further professional development.

Some educational philosophies are short and sweet, while others are one to two pages long and have more detail. Shorter versions are appropriate for a quick summary on a classroom website or resume.

Basic examples of educational philosophies

Every teacher is different — and so are their educational philosophies!

Dr. Josh Prieur, director of educational efficacy at Prodigy Education, notes that "as you develop your philosophy of education, a best practice is to lean on research-based best practices and understand how to leverage technology and other resources appropriately."

His advice is to think of the big picture and imagine all the things surrounding a student, whether it's social and emotional learning, promoting equity in the classroom or integrating technology.

As a teacher, you should be able to articulate the research and theories you believe in. "You'll write many educational philosophies, and you should constantly revisit them," says Prieur. "It really is fundamental to who you are as an educator."

Sample teaching philosophies to help you create your own

Structure and repetition is key. Teachers should work from well-organized plans and schedules in a consistent manner so students have a supportive learning environment.

Teachers must hold students to high expectations. Every student has the ability to succeed, given the right teaching methods, resources and support. It's the teacher's job to encourage students to be diligent and strive for growth in their learning.

Students need effective tools and resources. Teachers should have access to a wide variety of excellent learning and educational resources in order to fully support student learning.

Teachers should be great examples. A person in leadership has a responsibility to lead by example. This will cover many aspects, but teachers should model respect, discipline and problem-solving for their students.

Teachers offer the gift of learning. An educator's job is to guide students through the principles of learning and fulfill their need for education. A teacher's gift to their students should be motivating them to continue to learn, and helping them succeed in the process through good classroom management, solid educational theory and consistent teaching practices.

Learning goes beyond the classroom. Everyone, from parents to teachers to members of the community, has a role to play in developing a well-rounded education. Involving stakeholders in the education process in a meaningful way helps students understand multiple perspectives and build critical thinking skills.

Feedback, in both directions, is a key part of the learning process. While teachers generally give feedback to students in the form of assignments, regular communication and feedback can help improve teaching. Short feedback forms and creating a culture where students feel safe to speak out can improve the quality of learning for teachers and students.

Because there are so many different facets to teaching, many teachers have teaching statements made up of several paragraphs, with each paragraph organized around a key idea.

As you progress in your teaching career, it's natural for your beliefs and attitudes to change. Revisit your educational philosophy frequently to make sure it's still up to date and aligned with your current practices.

Questions to ask within your own philosophy

- You know how you want to teach, but it's not always easy to articulate your beliefs in writing. We've put together a list of questions you can ask yourself to help clarify your view and provide a starting point for your own teaching philosophy.
- What does effective learning look like in your classroom? Do you prioritize engagement? Learning for mastery?
- What kinds of goals do you set for your students? How do you encourage them? Do you set the goals, or do you ask for their input?
- How do you interact with students? What kind of relationship do you have with students? How do you build trust in the classroom?
- What types of assessment do you use? How do you determine mastery? Which assessment styles do you think are the most effective?
- What is the purpose of education in society? Is it for social justice, to build good citizens, to prepare students for life outside of school or something else?
- What qualities should good teachers possess? Patience, compassion and authority are all qualities you need as a teacher — but what's most important to you?
- What kind of learning environment do you want to create? Is your classroom individualized or

collaborative? Do you use a lot of technology, or prefer an analog approach?

- How do you approach differences in learning styles? Do you use differentiation, unique resources, tailored teaching methods or other pedagogical approaches to reach all students?
- What helps students learn effectively? This answer can change depending on whether you teach high school or elementary school, but what are your core teaching strategies? How flexible are you willing to be?
- What do you see as the teacher's role in learning? Is your teaching style more student-centered or teacher-centered? How does hands-on learning or techniques like inquiry-based learning fit into your classroom?

Your philosophy of education doesn't have to answer every single question. But it should give a big-picture perspective on who you are as a teacher, and what you value.

CHAPTER EIGHT

NECESSARY STEPS TO BECOME A SCHOOL PRINCIPAL

"A professional who leads a school and manages all the activities associated with the administration of a school is regarded as School Principal."

From maintaining the discipline to handling administrative, financial and academic activities of a school, it is the school principal who plays a dominant part. He/ she is also responsible for hiring teachers and play a vital role in promoting quality education. A school principal is also responsible for developing the school with innovative ideas and activities that attract not only students but also parents. Increasing the number of admissions with good administration lies with the school principal. Obtaining a relevant degree is not enough to become a school principal, and the candidates require necessary experience and skills. It is the most respectable position in society. For all those who are aspiring to become a school principal, we have explained the career path in a detailed manner.

Not everyone is meant to become a school principal. Some educators make the transition well while others figure out that it is more difficult than one might think. A school principal's day can be long and stressful. You have to be organized, solve problems, manage people well, and be able to separate your personal life from your professional life. If you cannot do those four things, you will not last long as a principal.

It takes a remarkable person to deal with all the negatives that you are forced to handle as a school principal. You listen to constant complaints from parents, teachers, and students. You have to deal with all kinds of discipline issues. You attend virtually every extra-curricular activity. If you have an ineffective teacher in your building, then it is your job to help them improve or get rid of them. If your test scores are low, it is ultimately a reflection of you.

So why would someone want to become a principal?

For those that are equipped to handle the day to day stresses, the challenge of running and maintaining a school can be rewarding. There is also an upgrade in pay which is a bonus. The most rewarding aspect is that you have a greater impact on the school as a whole. You are the school leader. As the leader, your daily decisions impact a larger number of students and teachers than you impacted as a classroom teacher. A principal who understands this reaps their rewards through daily growth and improvements from their students and teachers.

For those who decide that they want to become a principal, the following steps must be taken to reach that goal:

1. Earn a Bachelor's Degree – You must earn a three or four-year bachelor's degree from an accredited university. In some cases, it does not have to be an education degree as most states have an alternative certification program.

2. Obtain a Teaching License/Certification – Once you have earned a bachelor's degree in education then, most states require you to get licensed/certified. This is typically done by taking and passing a test or series of tests in your area of specialization. If you do not have a degree in education, then check your states' alternative certification requirements to obtain your teaching license/certification.

3. Gain Experience as a Classroom Teacher – Most states require you to teach a certain number of years before you are able to become a school principal. This is extremely important because most people need classroom experience to have an understanding of what goes on in a school on a day to day basis. Gaining this experience is essential to becoming an effective principal. In addition, it will be easier for teachers to relate to you and understand where you are coming from if you have classroom experience because they know you have been one of them.

4. Gain Leadership Experience – Throughout your time as a classroom teacher, look for opportunities to sit on and/or chair committees. Visit with your building principal and let them know that you are interested in becoming a principal. Chances are they will give you

some increased role to help prepare you for being in that role or at the very least you can pick their brain concerning principal best practices. Every bit of experience and knowledge will help when you land your first principal's job.

5. Earn a Master's Degree – Although most principals will earn a Master's degree in an area such as educational leadership, there are states that allow you to become a principal with a combination of any master's degree, the required teaching experience, along with passing the license/certification process. Most people will continue to teach full time while taking master's courses part time until they earn their degree. Many school administration masters' programs now cater to teacher's offering one night a week courses. The summer can be used to take additional classes to expedite the process. The final semester typically involves an internship with hands-on training that will give you a snapshot of what a principal's job actually entails.

6. Obtain a School Administrator License/Certification – This step is remarkably similar to the process for getting your teacher license/certification. You must pass a test or series of tests related to the specific area you want to be a principal in whether that be an elementary, a middle level, or a high school principal.

7. Interview for a Principal's Job – Once you have earned your license/certification, then it is time to start looking for a job. Do not be discouraged if you do not land one as quickly as you thought. Principal's jobs are intensely competitive and can be difficult to land. Go into every interview confident and prepared. As you interview, remember that as they are interviewing you, you are interviewing them. Do not settle for a job. You do not

want a job at a school which you do not genuinely want with all the stress a principal's job can bring. While searching for a principal's job, gain valuable administrator experience by volunteering to help out your building principal. More than likely they will be willing to allow you to continue on in an internship type of role. This type of experience will boost your resume and give you terrific on the job training.

8. Land a Principal's Job – Once you get an offer and have accepted it, the real fun begins. Come in with a plan but remember that no matter how well you feel you have been prepared, there will be surprises. There are new challenges and issues that arise each and every day. Never get complacent. Continue to search for ways to grow, do your job better, and make improvements to your building.

Job Description for Principals

A school principal is in charge of all the operations at their school: they oversee teachers, coordinate curricula, plan and manage school events, maintain a budget, and keep the environment safe and conducive to learning.

This is a role with a lot of power, but with that comes a lot of responsibility, specifically to the state and federal standards. Principals and administrators are in a great position to shape the way their school operates and make a change, but they're also beholden to requirements for their students' performance on tests and their teachers ability to drive those test scores.

Some schools allocate assistant principals to help share duties, which can be as nitty gritty as hiring cafeteria workers, or as big picture as enforcing attendance policies. Administrators will also need to draw on their knowledge of teaching for tasks like mediating parent-teacher meetings, observing classrooms, and evaluating teacher performance. They work full-time, year-round because while everyone else goes home, they're the ones responsible for writing up reports on student test scores, or drafting next semester's class schedules.

It can be a challenging, highly visible job, but the role of principal has plenty of task variety and offers the satisfaction of making real change. If lesson plans and lunchtime quiz grading has got you down, the high risk, high reward role of administration might be a good fit for you.

Philosophy of Education

In today's society, education is a top priority. The fundamental purpose of schooling is student learning, and all children have the right to a quality education. An ideal school consists of a community of learners whose main focus is student achievement. The school is considered a caring community, and has a specific moral purpose. High standards are set, and high achievement is demanded. Staff members establish high expectations for all students, and provide the support necessary for them to achieve their goals.

Effective schools have effective leaders. An effective leader demands respect and honesty from themselves, their staff, and their students. They transmit a well-defined set of goals to staff, students, parents, and the community. They are always working to improve the school.

Having a vision for a school is essential. The vision should include high standards of learning and continuous school improvement. The school staff must share in this vision. A shared vision is very powerful, and will help to create an environment of low anxiety and high standards. A school must also have a clear, shared mission. Research and data analysis should be used to help shape the mission of the school. Staff, students, parents, and community members should all take part in developing this mission, and it should be widely shared and understood.

A positive school climate is crucial to its success. The atmosphere of a school should be one of caring and trust. The school should be a supportive environment that is conducive to learning. Both students and staff should feel comfortable and safe at their school. Positive interpersonal relationships also help create a positive school culture. These relationships are fostered when both staff and students are encouraged to work collaboratively. An effective staff will work together to create a safe and supportive learning environment.

The students are the most important members of a school community. Under the appropriate conditions and with the appropriate strategies, all students can and will learn. The nature and quality of learning experiences must be exemplary. Creative thinking and analyzing skills are important in today's technological society. Students must gain critical thinking skills along with knowledge. They must be taught how to learn and how to apply what they learn. Student performance must be evaluated frequently. Achievement data should be analyzed and instruction should be planned accordingly. All of these efforts will help students succeed.

Children need constant support and guidance and their welfare should be our focus. They should be valued, respected, nurtured, and supported. Encouragement and praise are strong motivators and may be just what they need to succeed. Children must learn and develop both academically and socially, and we must work hard to prepare them for adulthood.

Besides school staff members, parents and community members can play a huge role in ensuring the success of students. School should solicit the active involvement of parents and community leaders in school functions. Community resources should be sought out and used often. Collaboration and communication with families and the community are crucial to the success of a school. Parents can provide valuable and necessary information and they must be valued and respected. They should be welcomed and encouraged to become involved in their child's education. Opportunities should be provided for parents to work with their children in learning settings. An open line of communication will help build trust and collaboration between school and home.

In an effective school, staff members should feel like they are a part of a great team that works together for the success of their students. Teachers should be valued and respected for their knowledge of and experience with children. Their efforts should be acknowledged and appreciated. Good teachers are well-read and critical learners that are up to date on the latest teaching strategies and educational issues. Their top priority should be the success of their students. They should be provided with the materials and tools necessary to implement an effective instructional program.

An effective school leader must work hard to support collegiality among staff members. Staff members must be kept informed and consistently supported. Groups and committees should be created and given responsibilities. Staff members along with all other stakeholders should share in decision making when possible and appropriate. Empowered managers should be cherished and feel appreciated. A happy staff that feels supported and needed is often a productive staff.

Professional development is vital to teacher effectiveness. It should be meaningful and helpful to teachers. It should include information on the changing role of the teacher, the latest developments in the area of instruction, and reflective practice techniques to assist teachers in self-improvement. Good staff development will help teachers address the diverse needs of their students and help to improve their professional skills.

A school leader has the greatest ability to make a school successful. There are many personal qualities that effective school leaders must possess. They must have a strong sense of self, personal discipline, and the educational process. Effective leaders are well-rounded, knowledgeable individuals with strong problem solving skills. They have good moral character and conduct themselves with pride, fairness, and integrity. Ethics, performance, and quality are never compromised.

School leaders must have high expectations and strive for greatness. They must focus on leading as well as managing. They must be both a good business manager and an effective instructional leader. A balance must be found between instructional leadership, routine administration, and human relations. Time is limited, and must be used effectively, with priorities set on instructionally related matters. Effective leaders foster open communication, decision-making, and problem solving. They are able to lead people toward personal and organizational goals.

School leaders must also be highly visible, and more skilled at listening than telling. They must have the courage and determination to overcome difficulties. Decisions must be made keeping in mind what is in the best interest of the students, the staff, and the school. Ethical principals should be involved in the decision-making process.

School principals should be lead-learners by continuously participating in and providing professional development. They must make a serious commitment to life-long learning for themselves and their staff. They must constantly renew and improve their knowledge and skills. They must be willing to take risks when necessary for the welfare of the school. They must also allow and encourage their staff members to take risks for the good of their students.

I feel very strongly that the relationship an administrator has with his/her staff is a key component of an effective school. I will continue to work hard to ensure that my relationships with my staff are positive. I will trust and respect them in order to gain their trust and respect.

As a school leader, I have dedicated myself to improving the educational experiences of my staff and students. I am constantly working to build a successful school community. Through collaboration, hard work, and determination, I am certain that my school, staff, and students will succeed.

Responsibilities and duties of a principle:

- The hiring of staff members
- Communicating with parents and faculty when necessary
- Creating policies (such as dress code)
- Planning academic calendars for the school
- Handling of student recruitment and admissions into the school
- Disciplining students when needed
- Supervising students, staff, and other faculty members
- Designing creative new programs and restructuring old ones
- Handling of the schools budget
- Maintaining secure funding for the school
- Making both daily decisions as well as long-term decisions

CHAPTER NINE

VISION OF TEACHER EDUCATION

Teacher education has to become more sensitive to the emerging demands from the school system. For this, it has to prepare teachers for a dual role of;

- Encouraging, supportive and humane facilitator in teaching learning situations who enables learners (students) to discover their talents, to realize their physical and intellectual potentialities to the fullest, to develop character and desirable social and human values to function as responsible citizens; and,

- An active member of the group of persons who make conscious effort to contribute towards the process of renewal of school curriculum to maintain its relevance to the changing societal needs and personal needs of learners, keeping in view the experiences gained in the past and the concerns and imperatives that have emerged in the light of changing national development goals and educational priorities.

These expectations suggest that teacher operates in a larger context and its dynamics as well as concerns impinge upon her functioning. That is to say, teacher has to be responsive and sensitive to the social contexts of education, the various disparities in the background of learners as well as in the macro national and global contexts, national concerns for achieving the goals of equity, parity, social justice as also excellence.

To be able to realize such expectations, TE has to comprise such features as would enable the student teachers to

- Care for children, and who love to be with them;
- Understand children within social, cultural and political contexts;
- View learning as a search for meaning out of personal experience;
- Understand the way learning occurs, possible ways of creating conductive conditions for learning, differences among students in respect of the kind, pace and styles of learning.
- View knowledge generation as a continuously evolving process of reflective learning.
- Be receptive and constantly learning. View learning as a search for meaning out of personal experience, and knowledge generation as a continuously evolving process of reflective learning.
- View knowledge not as an external reality embedded in textbooks, but as constructed in the shared context of teachinglearning and personal experience.
- Own responsibility towards society, and work to build a better world.

- Appreciate the potential of productive work and hands-on experience as a pedagogic medium both inside and outside the classroom.
- Analyze the curricular framework, policy implications and texts. Have a sound knowledge base and basic proficiency in language.

The objectives of teacher education would therefore be to,

Provide opportunities to observe and engage with children, communicate with and relate to children Provide opportunities for self-learning, reflection, assimilation and articulation of new ideas; developing capacities for self directed learning and the ability to think, be self-critical and to work in groups. Provide opportunities for understanding self and others (including one's beliefs, assumptions and emotions); developing the ability for self analysis, self-evaluation, adaptability, flexibility, creativity and innovation. Provide opportunities to enhance understanding, knowledge and examine disciplinary knowledge and social realities, relate subject matter with the social milieu and develop critical thinking. Provide opportunities to develop professional skills in pedagogy, observation, documentation, analysis, drama, craft, story-telling and reflective inquiry.

CHAPTER TEN

DEVELOPING RELATIONSHIPS WITH PARENTS

Developing Positive Relationships With Parents

Twenty Tips for Developing Positive Relationships with Parents

In our busy day of juggling papers, lesson planning and managing sometimes more than a hundred students, we can easily forget the group that could lend significant support in our charge as teachers -- parents and families. Consider these tips for improving connections with this valuable group:

1. Smile When You See Parents

Greet them. Most parents only occasionally interact with teachers so make sure that at least 90 percent of your encounters with them are positive, warm, and friendly. The impressions left from fleeting encounters in the hallway last a long time.

2. Learn Their Names

(If you have a self-contained class.) Learn how they like to be addressed (Mr. ____? Paul? By their first name?) and how to pronounce them correctly.

3. Declare Your Intention

Tell them that you want to partner with them, that you appreciate their support, and look forward to working together.

4. Communicate Often and in Various Forms

Provide information about what's going on in your class (weekly would be ideal): what students are learning, what they've accomplished, what you're excited about, what they're excited about, and the learning and growth you're seeing. Suggest things that they might ask their child about: "Ask them to tell you about what they learned last week about meal worms," or "Ask them to read you the haiku they wrote."

5. Make a Positive Phone Call Home

If you have a self-contained class, call all homes within the first couple of weeks and then at regular intervals throughout the year. If you teach many students, identify those students who perhaps need a positive call home.

6. Lead with the Good News

Give positive praise first when calling parents or meeting with them to discuss a concern. Every kid has something good about him/her. Find it. Share it. Then share your concern. Adhere strictly to this rule.

7. Find a Translator

If you can't speak their language, seek a translator for at least one parent conference and/or phone call. (For obscure languages, you can sometimes find a refugee center or other public agency that can help). Reach out to those parents as well; do whatever you can to connect.

8. Your Language is Powerful

It communicates an awareness that there are many different kinds of families. Be careful not to assume a mother is, or isn't married, or even that if she is married, she's married to a man. Learn to ask open-ended questions and understand that sometimes parents/guardians might not want to share some information.

9. Ask Questions about the Child

"What kinds of things does he enjoy doing outside of school? Who are the special people in her life -- family or family friends? What do you think are her best characteristics? What was he like as a little boy?" Demonstrate an interest in knowing your student.

10. Listen to Parents

Really listen. They know a whole lot about their kid.

11. Smile at the Child When talking to a parent in front of a child, smile and make eye contact with the student to demonstrate that you care about him/her. Recognize what he/she has done well in your class in front of the parents. Then share a concern, if you have one.

12. Invite Parents to Share

Distribute a survey at the beginning of the year (if parents don't read/write in English, students can interview them and relay their answers). Find out what parents know about and what skills they have. Invite them in especially if it connects the curriculum and content. Let them share with you their cultural traditions, interests, passions, skills, knowledge.

13. Let Parents Know How They Can Help

Many want to help but especially as kids get older, parents aren't asked for help as often and don't know what to do. There's always some way they can help in the classroom.

14. Be Very Specific

Provide ways parents can support their child at home: "You can help your child with her math homework by asking her to explain how she got an answer," or "As you're reading stories at night, ask your child to make predictions. This strengthens reading comprehension."

15. Be a Broker of Resources

If they share a concern, be prepared to point them to a direction where they can find help. If you share a concern ("Your daughter spaces out and doesn't pay attention") be prepared to suggest what the parents can do.

16. Explain Your Instructional Decisions

Take the time to do this and help them learn about the education system if they're not familiar with it. Help them understand what you're doing and why.

17. Invite Parents to Participate in Making Some Decisions

Invite their input, give them information that will help them form an opinion, and listen to their conclusions.

18. Thank Parents

Both individually and publicly for their support, perhaps in your weekly newsletter. Recognize what they do to help your class and how it's impacting students.

19. Share Every Success

Let parents know what their child is doing well, what academic skills, social skills or knowledge he's mastered.

20. Invite Parents to Celebrate and Break Bread Together

Communities are strengthened when people come together in celebration. Start the year with a potluck. Share food and stories about food. We all bond over food.

CHAPTER ELEVEN

ACADEMIC STRESS

Academic stress is at an all-time high for students from elementary school through college. From curriculum-based pressures like studying for exams, completing homework, and writing reports, to overwhelm and burnout from overloaded schedules and diverse and often unmet learning needs, students are buckling under the weight of high academic expectations combined with fast-paced lifestyles.

If you are a student feeling the pressure, or if you are the parent or friend of a student who is showing signs of academic stress, here are 10 tips from student Hailey Fuchs to help ease the pressure and find more school/life balance:

Academic Stress Management Tips

1. Make To Do Lists

To do lists can take a seemingly insurmountable pile of obligations much more manageable by helping prioritize and lay out exactly what needs to be done. Outline the set of tasks that you have to complete. Once you can visualize what you have to do, you won't be daunted by your assignments.

2. Budget Your Time

Plan out your day, minute-by-minute. With a clear view of your schedule, you will feel more in control which will allow you to approach your tasks calmly and confidently.

   3. Create a Rewards System

Giving yourself incentives to complete daunting academic tasks can help when the going gets tough. Set up a system of rewards so that you can look forward to finishing a set of tasks. For instance, give yourself a Hershey Kiss once you read 10 pages of your textbook. This little boost of endorphins will give you the encouragement to keep working.

   4. Ask For Help and Move On

When you find yourself stressing over a seemingly impossible problem, text a friend or email a teacher. Then move on to other tasks. Don't spend hours focusing on this problem, however significant it may seem to be at the time. Wasted time will slow you down, and you will be emotionally drained when preparing to shift your focus to your other remaining tasks.

   5. Take Breaks to Breathe

Mindfulness is an immense help when experiencing overwhelm and academic stress. Finding a way to calm yourself physically will help relief mental stress simultaneously. Go online and find some breathing exercises. Whenever you find yourself worrying, put your pens and pencils down and breathe. Try closing your eyes while breathing in through your nose and out through your mouth. Moments like these are necessary to recharge.

   6. Eat Healthy

While you may be tempted to reach for that slice of pizza, putting the right foods in your body will boost your energy and thereby give you the stamina you need to get your work done. Foods with high fat and sugar contents can make you feel sluggish and unmotivated to complete your tasks. Focus on fruits, veggies, and other high-fiber foods for sustained energy, and combine protein with carbohydrates to avoid a 'crash'.

7. Get More Restful Sleep, Especially If You Can't Get More Hours of Sleep

Obviously, you won't be able to focus or work your best without a good night's sleep. While I understand that sometimes sleep is the first thing to go when school work is piled high, there are a few tips to make the most of those precious hours of slumber. First, don't do your work on your bed; it will lead to an association between your bed and your work, which will make it harder for you to fall asleep. Do the homework that does not require screen time last. Exposure to screens before bed has been proven to decrease quality of sleep. If you find yourself worrying while you are trying to snooze, try clenching each muscle in your body one-by-one, starting with your feet, until you clench your entire body. Then release. This relief will make your body feel de-stressed and will allow you to fall asleep faster.

8. Exercise

Experts say that everyone needs at least a half hour of exercise each day. Not only does exercise help you with restful sleep but exercise also boosts endorphins, which, in turn, make you more happy and less anxious.

9. Set Aside Days to Relax

Just like a good night of sleep, you need a day of fun to recharge from a week of school. Set aside time to spend Friday or Saturday with friends or family. Do not focus on anything relating to work or school during these times. It can be tempting to work all the time, especially if academic stress is at a peak, but you will work more efficiently and effectively with breaks to rest and socialize as opposed to burning yourself out.

10. Seek Help If Necessary

If you find that academic stress has consumed your life, talk to a teacher, guidance counselor, parent, or another trusted adult. While a certain amount of anxiety is normal, no one should worry alone, and prolonged academic stress can lead to mental health struggles like anxiety and depression.

CHAPTER TWELVE

ACADEMIC PRESSURE FROM PARENTS - SIGNS AND EFFECTS

Academic excellence has always been a symbol of pride and status in our society; however, it is a class divide among children that is completely driven by the adults. It's bad enough that their future holds a cut-throat world where success is measured by how much money they make, on top that, undue parental pressure on children to score high marks and show excellence in every subject makes their mind a boiling pot ready to burst.

Parents, of course, envision a bright and happy future for their children, and the knowledge of how competitive it is out there, makes them push their wards to do well in every field. However, growing parental pressure on children's academic excellence has become an area of grave concern. The number of suicides among children and the youth has increased exponentially, in recent years. Though

Indian kids are spared off peer pressure unlike in the West, most of these suicides result from falling short of academic expectations set by their parents.

Why Do Parents Put Pressure on Their Children?

The dismal condition of our education system and the swelling volume of applicants each year is a stress point for most parents. Educational institutes are always in the lookout for the best and the brightest of the students to maintain their rankings, which ultimately percolates to the children in form of parental pressure. Protecting their child from a lifetime of regrets and heart-breaking rejections are a parent's prerogative, however, sometimes they raise the stakes too high for children to cope up. Social standing is a big cause of parental pressure. Caring more about how the world perceives them, can render parents ignorant about the true talents of their children. Parents often generalise the definition of success and excellence, depending on how others are doing. Not only in academics, but children are also frequently bogged down by expectations in areas of their own interests like arts, music, theatre, especially in sports. Parental pressure in sports is unfortunately common, which ultimately makes children give up on their talents. Competitive exams, institutional elitism, and the race for a plush job have created an unhealthy culture in which children are getting stunted instead of flourishing.

Signs of Parental Pressure on Kids

Though based on good intentions, parental pressure is often mistaken as care and can have serious consequences on children. A little bit of extra attention can reveal alarming behavioural signs:

The Tell-Tale Signs of Parental Pressure in a Child

1. Nightmares

Children often reflect their fears in sleep. Examination fever or not being able to get sound sleep could be signs of parental pressure.

2. Seclusion & Cheating

Children under stress are more likely to shut everyone out. If a child stops talking about school or ignores to share important information like mark sheets, examination schedule, or school grades, it could be because they are scared to let their parents down. This fear can make children resort to unhealthy practices like cheating in examinations.

3. Lethargy & Loss of Interest

Constant fear of falling short of parental expectations can be tiring, leaving a child lethargic and disinterested. It is definitely a red flag if your child loses interest in an extra-curricular activity which he/she otherwise enjoyed. It could cause physiological symptoms too, like, stomach pain, headaches, diarrhoea, among others.

4. Late Hours

Parental pressure can push children into a panic-mode, keeping them stay up late into the night to achieve what is expected of them. It often hampers their retention power making the whole activity futile.

5. Bad Temper

When a well-behaved child suddenly starts to fly off the handle at slightest of instigation, it is time to pay attention to his stress levels. It is as true for adults as it is for children that stress causes anger. If the child feels that his efforts are not good enough for his parents, it can cause a great deal of stress resulting into bad temper.

Impact of Parental Pressure on Children

The signs that your child might be under parental pressure are not as prominent as signs of stress in adults.

Unlike adults, children are not vocal about these symptoms mostly because they are conditioned into thinking that it is their failure that is causing the stress. Long-term subjugation of children to parental pressure can push them beyond recovery.

The Effects of Parental Pressure on Children

Here are a few dangerous effects of parental pressure on children:

1. Prone to Mental Disease

Children who go unnoticed while dealing with an internal tussle between expectations and capabilities, are more likely to succumb to mental diseases. Students often slip into depression or other diseases related to the mind, not knowing how to deal with it due to constant goal-setting by their parents.

2. Self-Harm

Children, especially during their teens, often resort to self-harming activities to deal with parental pressure. Studies show that children contemplate suicide as an answer to deal with parental disappointment due to low scores in examinations. In India, especially, deaths caused due to suicide is unnaturally common among students, and no one needs to look farther than the news reports received right after exam results, to realise this truth.

3. Low Self-Esteem

Children mostly look at their parents for validation on everything they do, but if they meet with constant criticism from the other side, it most likely will create a negative self-image in them. This negative perception can transform into self-hate and hinder children from growing into well-adjusted adults.

4. Defensive Attitude

Constant parental pressure can create a defensive attitude in children. Fear of failure can stop them from taking up new projects or completing the ones at hand. It can create unhealthy defiance in them that can lead to dissatisfied adulthood.

5. Risk of Permanent Injuries

Children, who are made to bear the burden of excessive parental pressure while dealing with the physically and mentally taxing requirements of professional sports, are more likely to push themselves over the threshold. They tend to ignore the pain and hurt, causing permanent injuries.

As a parent, it is important that you create a healthy space for your child to flourish and excel in life. It is for you to discover your child's strengths and guide him/her on how to enhance their talents. It is not necessary for each child to achieve academic excellence. Success is inevitable if you give your child the required support to pursue their dreams in whichever field they want, without instilling the fear of failure in them.

Why Should Parents Stop Comparing Their Child to Others

Many parents compare their children to other kids with the intention of motivating them to excel. But comparing a child with other kids can have the opposite effect and the child who is being compared may feel low as it may hurt their self-esteem. The spirit of competitiveness is good in children and it can motivate them to do good and be good, but teaching them to be better than other kids can sometimes prove to be counterproductive. It causes deep-set emotional bruises which are difficult to heal and can result in aggression, antagonism, and resentment. All these qualities are detrimental to the gradual growth and progress of children.

Why Do Parents Compare Their Children to Others?

Parents dream of seeing their children accomplishing success in all endeavours but little do they realise that this can never be achieved by comparing kids. It is quite a prevalent practise for parents to make every possible effort to bolster the performance of the child. They feel that this will enhance children's learning and skills, but on the contrary, it affects their confidence level negatively.

What Parents Need to Understand Before Comparing Their Kids to Others

The sole reason why parents compare their kids to others is to instigate the spirit of competition. They might feel that it is the right way to bring out the latent potential and capabilities in their little ones to excel over others. But parents need to understand that comparison is not the only driving force to enable kids to perform their best. Each individual is unique and blessed with different strengths. Kids' interests and talents bloom at a varied pace. If parents constantly keep expressing their displeasure or unhappiness for their kids' poor performance, it will break and not build their self-confidence. Some other points that parents need to understand are given below:

1. Children Should Think on Their Own

Parents must spare some time to listen to their children. They must try to understand their thought process. As individual human beings, as soon as kids learn to express their likes and dislikes, they should only be guided and not be influenced by anyone's thoughts and opinions. Children should be allowed to think critically and take decisions on their own, which is how they will develop mutual trust, respect, and love.

2. Children Are Not Decorative Pieces

Children should not be treated as accessories by parents. They cannot be treated as objects to show off in social circles. By setting unrealistic goals, they tend to exploit their own children and bring disappointment for themselves and ruin the lives of their own kids. They should be treated with respect as independent individuals and need to be loved and understood.

3. Education Is Not a Special Favour But a Right

Some parents think that they have done their kids a favour by putting them in good and expensive schools. Acquiring education is every kid's right, and it is the responsibility of the parents to provide education. Parents should understand that the primary goal of the best education is to create responsible and self-reliant individuals and not qualify them for acquiring a job and earn money.

Family, friends, aspirations & hopes is what a soul lives for. We dream to make it big one day, and so does our parents hope us to see on the heights of success. Our parents play an important role in nurturing us, they invest in us, provide us with the best education, fulfill all our need even if they had to sacrifice their requirements. Parents serve as a major influence in their children's career development. Parents want their children to find happiness and success in life and one factor which influences happiness and success is career choice. Research also indicates that when students feel supported and loved by their parents, they can be more relaxed at mind and focused towards their goals. Parents play the biggest role in our development. They play important role in our mental, physical, social, financial and career development. They help us in every step of our life, they trained us very hard style for the future challenges. Parents are living for us, they are real God and our first teacher parenting a child is not easy. But what happens when our parents pressurize us with their high hopes. How do we deal with their expectations?

Pressure and stress caused by our parents

India has one of the highest suicide rates among teenagers and adults between the ages of 14 and 29. Failure in examinations is among the top 10 reasons for suicide in the country while family problems among the top three. Even in cases where suicide is not on the child's mind, due to parental pressure– people who are charged with nurturing and caring for the child – leads to a number of psychological issues, manifesting in different stages of youth and adulthood.

1) Psychological impact on children

One of the highest suicide rates amid teenagers and adults is in India. The common reasons are failure in examinations, high expectations and pressure coming from parents. Excessive pressure from parents can even lead to a number of psychological problems, manifesting in diverse stages of adolescence and adulthood.

2) All-rounder children

With the growth of sports and entertainment as high-income businesses in India, most of the people have turned their focus towards these fields. Most parents still are unable to ward off the need to pursue academics constantly. ,Because of the inevitable competition in every field, parents push their children to become all-rounders and children end up as victim, and go into depression.

3) Academics vs Sports vs Arts

Failure to recognize learning disabilities like dyslexia and seeing academic failure to be the end of life are the two biggest failures of the modern parenting and education system.

The activities which are imperative for growth and destressing in children are the sports and physical activities. Instead of inspiring enthusiasm of children for these activities, Competitive parents make it worse with shaming kids and comparing them to others.

Dance, arts, music, sports and other activities are brilliant choices to inspire the creativity in children. They teach focus, discipline and team work in them. Unfortunately, parental pressure has turned these enjoyable activities into competitive events resulting in immense stress on children.

How to deal with the parental pressure?

Put some distance between you and the rest. If you're living in the same house with your parents or grandparents and you see them every day, it's hard not to succumb to their pressure. Make moving out at priority, save the money it takes and do it.

Realize you don't need to please your family. There is this false belief that because you family is, well... your family, you must get along perfectly with every family member. You don't.. There's nothing wrong with upsetting dad once in a while or not living up to mom's dream for you to be a doctor. You need to realize you passion. Its you who has to live your life not them. Feel free to do what you want if you see yourself doing the right thing

Learn to communicate assertively. Assertive communication is one the most valuable people skills you can have. It allows you to express yourself in a vivid, direct way, but from a position of respect for others, and it's a great way to deal with all the criticizing and negative comments you can get from family members which are not happy with your actions. Learn to put your point forward .

Be clear with what you want.

Ask for help. Its not always important to do everything on your own . You can ask for help, guidance, supervision from anyone you feel comfortable to talk to . It doesn't always have to be your family member, it could be anyone – an older friend, a mentor, your teacher or a counselor.

Negative Impacts of Child Comparison

Even when parents want to refrain from comparing their kids to others, they, unfortunately, end up doing so. Though it seems to be an inevitable human trait, parents need to restrain that impulse. Children do not respond well to negative criticism, and comparison to others is even more debasing. The negative impact of comparison is as given below:

1. Increases Sibling Rivalry

If parents compare elder kids to their younger siblings, it will foster rivalry, and the older kids might then start teasing, fighting, hitting and behaving aggressively with the younger ones.

2. Instils Detachment

When children are compared to their siblings, friends or cousins, they feel insecure and try to maintain distance from their parents. It can also lead to behavioural or developmental problems later on as they mature.

3. Suppresses Talents

When kids are not appreciated and are constantly compared to others, their talent will not bloom, and they will eventually lose the potential and talent both.

4. Leads to Carefree Attitude

If kids notice their parents appreciating other kids more, they will feel ignored and will never try to please their parents.

5. Increases Hesitation and Impacts Social Interactions

If kids receive constant ridicule and taunts from their parents, they will gradually start avoiding public interaction in the presence of the parents.

6. Diminishes Self Worth

Children's self-confidence is affected when they are compared to other children. If a child feels that they are 'good for nothing', it can deteriorate their performance even further.

7. Destroys Self-Esteem

Kids' growth gets hampered when they start believing they are not capable of performing well. They will always think that they will never be able to match up to the expectations of their parents.

8. Builds Stress

Parents must not pressurise their children to perform and burden them with extreme expectations. They should instead find solutions and help kids get over their reservations by communicating with them.

What Are the Positive Comparison Approaches That Can Help Children?

Negative criticism is a detrimental factor in children's growth and development. Certain ways of positive comparison are given below:

1. Give Unconditional Love and Support

Appreciation in public will boost kids' morales. Children should be spoken to respectfully and given lots of love and support.

2. Set Realistic Expectations

Parents must not commit the mistake of setting unrealistic goals for their children. They should instead try to understand the inherent potential of their kids and help them excel in their fields of interest.

3. Appreciate the Strengths

Whatever task kids do well should be appreciated generously. Liberal appreciation will help them gain the confidence to face the world.

4. Help Children Cope With Their Weaknesses

When parents know their kids' weak areas, they must support and help the kids to help them overcome their weaknesses. Though it is not easy, it can be achieved with unconditional support and motivation.

5. Do Not Compare; Rather Set Benchmarks

If parents set realistic benchmarks rather than criticising their children, they will see a considerable improvement in their performance. At this stage, building confidence and self-worth are of utmost importance.

The trait of comparing and competing is more common among parents than children. The undue pressure of performance is most degrading for kids and produces a negative outcome. Parents must not rob the joy out of their kids' life and allow them the space to grow and prove their merit. No one is perfect at encompassing excellence in all the fields of performance, be it sports or academics. But a positive approach and motivating kids without comparing them with other kids can help them do good and become confident and successful individuals.

As a teenager you are forced to deal with a vast array of stress inducing factors that can tend to make you want to pull your hair out. Add parental pressure into the mix and you may end up just wanting to run away all together! Take a look at our top 5 tips on how to deal with pressure from parents.

1. Identify the reasons why you are being pressured

Your parents do in fact want what is best for you. If they could, they would go and write your exams for you, but they cannot and this results in them hovering over you and trying to organize your study schedule, exam practice lessons and so forth. Much as this academic pressure from your parents may drive you insane, take a minute and realize that they mean well. Have an open discussion about your stress and how they are impacting on it. They may just surprise you with their understanding.

2. Do Research

It may seem unfathomable to add more "work" to your current schedule, but trust us this is worth your time. If you are struggling with a certain subject at school or personal issue look it up. The internet is filled with helpful hints and tips and you will find some valuable advice from other teenagers who have been where you are now. Use this information to add to your discussion with your parents.

3. Remain Calm

We all want to "flip our lid" from time to time, but this simply does not go down well with the parental units. When we act irrationally and out of anger or fear, we unfortunately come across as childish and petty, and this does not bring positive results. If you are able to talk in a calm and mature manner with your parents, they will take you seriously.

4. Know what you are fighting for:

Remember that your argument is your parents adding extra stress and academic pressure to your life, and not the myriad of other social issues and anxieties that you are also going through. Keep on track when you are sharing your feelings and your point will not only be made, but taken seriously.

5. Be willing to Compromise:

Much as you feel you "know it all" and know exactly what you need, the fact is your parents have been playing this game of life longer than you have. They do know a few things and if you are willing to compromise and find a middle ground, you will afford yourself a greater chance of getting what you want, or at least pretty close to it.

COMFORT YOUR CHILD

Comfort your child instead of criticising them for their exam results.

We all know that exams are for the betterment of a child's future and parents try to be supportive during that period. Parents encourage their children by providing nutrition and motivation, but sometimes they use certain phrases and questions unconsciously that can be upsetting for the child. These phrases can affect children's minds by making them more anxious about their performance than necessary. These phrases might seem motivating to parents but are not motivating for the child.

A student's days of stress are not over with exams. The bigger hurdle to overcome is the exam result day, especially when children are scared to face their parents knowing they might not be happy with their marks. Criticising the results or complaining about the performance can, however, have a negative impact on the child instead of motivating them to do better.

Let's try and avoid some of these phrases:

1. 'How did your friend get more marks than you?'

This is an oft-heard comment from many Indian parents, who compare their child's marks with that of their other classmates. Parents need to realise that constant comparison with peers may not do any good to the child. Instead, it can make your child lose confidence and question his or her self-worth, which is surely not desirable. It can also lead to jealousy.

2. 'Is this why we are spending so much on your education?'

Education is the basic right of every child. The choice of the school does not usually depend on the child but the parents who aim to make their little one into the "perfect" kid who is never lagging behind. Try to focus on your child's studies instead and help him or her to do better next time.

3. 'You will never achieve anything in life with these marks'

It is really damaging to make such statements about your child or it can further bring down his or her morale and impact their performance further. Talk to your child, find out about the challenges he or she is facing and help overcome them.

4. 'You are a failure'

In this mad rush to get the child to excel in every field, parents sometimes are unable to accept their child's defeat or failure. In the process, children are also not taught to deal with failure. A 2013 study by Arizona State University researchers had found that children, who are put under too much pressure to succeed, are twice as likely to suffer from anxiety and depression as compared to their peers. Marks cannot be the only yardstick for success. Instead of criticising your child, acknowledge their efforts and empathise with them.

5. 'No TV, internet from now on'

Your child should not be allowed too much screen-time, of course, but that does not mean you shun it completely. In fact the television or internet can be used as a source of relevant information and knowledge. You can read about new things or watch age-appropriate educative shows with your child.

6. "Exams do not matter in the long run, don't worry"

This phrase might confuse the child making them wonder that if exams hardly matter why are they even sitting and preparing for them. It can also be interpreted as if parents don't believe in their child's abilities. Do you get the idea? We don't mean to say that all children feel like this, but this is a huge possibility. It can be demotivating and can further become the reason for exam anxiety. So, let us avoid saying this.

7. "If you don't do well in the exam then..."

How can any child predict what the result is going to be? A number of parents say things like, "If you don't do well you're going to let us down", "if you don't score well you'll never succeed" or " if you don't do well you'll never get admission in good colleges." These things are not okay to be said before the exam period. You can try to to let your children know the importance of education in a different, more positive and non-threatening manner but saying such things during examination time can lead to overthinking. We must understand that nobody wants to let him/her self down by failing in an exam. Every child has an ambition and they work accordingly to achieve it. They want to perform well. These phrases, if repeated, can add more anxiety, hurt, or guilt in the child.

8. "You should be revising your syllabus again"

It is normal to be concerned about your child's success and preparation. Some parents are extra curious about their child's activity and keep on asking them to revise their syllabus again and again. Research proves that excessive revision is not required in order to score well. One must revise effectively; patterns and tables for revision schedule are easily available on internet platforms. In addition, if a child wants to score well, he/she knows better how much preparation he/she needs. So, pressurizing your child to stick to the books 24/7 is equal to burdening them.

9. "You must score more than your friends"

One of the major reasons for exam related depression in children is the comparison they receive with respect to other children through their parents. Pressurizing children to score more than everyone is like forcing your own expectations on them. Parents must understand that every child has his/her interests and capacity to learn, and expecting the utmost best results is an unrealistic expectation. It does not mean that your child should never be competitive, it only means that competition should not be forced upon them.

10. "It's not the time to rest!"

Studies have shown that studying during exam time is as draining for the body as any other workout and even more. Also, it is proven that breaks in between the learning process enhance the performance even more. So, next time you see you child resting for a bit, instead of saying "It's not the time to rest", say "Wow! You've finished learning, that's nice; I believe you take breaks after completing each segment of study." This way if your child has finished their syllabus, he/she will be motivated by your appreciation and if not, he/she will consider studying before taking another break.

Exam time is crucial for both parents and children, and both have very important roles to play. The main thing is the understanding between the child and the parent. A parent must be appreciative of the child's effort rather than pressurizing them. Watching out for wording is important for a parent during exam days as it's the most crucial time for the child. Positivity over pressure is always beneficial and produces better results.

CHAPTER FOURTEEN

TIPS

"Here are few tips for parents to help children relieve their anxieties:"

Exam tips for students. Create a secure space — friend, family member, coach or counsellor — where students can go to without being afraid of judgment or shame. Exam pressure can sometimes get overwhelming and will affect the day-to-day life of the student; therefore, sharing concerns may be of great help.

Parenting tips for exams: A good night's sleep is very important. Check your child's timetable to ensure they have enough time for a well-earned sleep. This will calm their nerves and keep them alert on the big day.

In our childhood, we were taught that studying hard and going by the book was the only way to move ahead in our career. And then came the era of E-Learning, which mixed education and technology and created something completely out of the box. Multinational companies have spent millions and billions in designing online courses to take classrooms out of schools and into homes. But is it the only solution to make education easier for your children? One cannot assume education to be the only factor to shape India's young minds for them to be the future Supermans in Science, Arithmetic, Geography, Arts, etc.

Even though technology has managed to ease the Indian education system, academic pressure and parental expectation on students hasn't changed. In fact, it has raised the expectation level a notch higher while increasing the pressure for students to perform, which may lead to wrong decisions or choices like alcohol, drugs, suicides, etc.

As per the National Mental Health Survey published by the National Institute of Mental Health And Neuro Sciences (NIMHANS), the suicide incidence rate per 1,00,000 population for the age group below 14 was 0.5, while those in the range of 14-17 years of age recorded a suicide incidence rate of 9.52 — higher than the national individual average of 0.9 per cent.

Meditation

Referring to the recent news of the Thailand cave rescue of young boys, meditation is the go to tool when it comes to handling stress and anxiety. One of the effective techniques in meditation is Vipassana, which is widely used to get rid of unnecessary pressure and stress. Schools, parents and all of us can set up regular meditation as part of the day. It's scientifically proven to bolster happiness.

No-Lose Environment

Create an environment of No-Lose at home and at school. If the students can be made to feel that they can approach problems and find solutions, they can take ownership of the solutions and work it out. Here you eliminate any feeling of making the students lose, thus empowering them.

Counselling

Create a secure space (friend, family member, coach or counsellor) where the students can go to without being afraid of judgment or shame. The pressure at some point in time can get overwhelming, and will affect the day-to-day life of the student; therefore, speaking to a counsellor, coach or friend might be of great help.

Maintain a balance

Introduce a balance in your children's lives with activities that they are passionate about along with academics, like music, dance, travel, sports and arts. Parents must motivate their children to participate in extra-curricular activities to make sure there is a right balance of studies and fun. As they say, "All work and no play makes Jack a dull boy".

Moderate screen time

In today's era, everyone is hooked to gadgets/TV/laptops. We have forgotten Mother Nature and her rewards. Spend time outdoors, in a natural environment, for instance walk, run or indulge in sports with your young ones. This can reduce tension, confusion, and depression for your children.

Family time

On the day of results or exams, the pressure to be the best is evident in their actions. Therefore, understanding their anxieties and comforting them with a family outing or a special dinner/movie time at home will be of great help. Accepting their flaws and appreciating their skills/abilities in the family will encourage children.

Support their decision

Academics are not just meant for subjects/books but there are extra-curriculum activities that encourage children to understand their career choice later. Don't let the child be a bookworm but let them explore their skills and abilities. Appreciate their decision and support them.

Stress is a product of pessimism and it's important to remember that students are not robots. If they are guided and encouraged by parents and teachers as per their abilities, interests and aptitude, the efforts will be rewarded with successful futures.

Your child needs your support during exams, whether it's just lending a patient ear or making sure they keep away from online distractions.

Here's how you can support children during exams:

Be familiar with your child's exam schedule

We know you're a busy parent, which is why some advance planning helps. Don't leave it to your son or daughter to inform you of their exam timings. Get a printout and pin it up where you can all see it and keep an online copy for reference, if required. This way, you know when they need to be dropped off at the exam centre.

Avoid arguments

If the bed isn't made, you're within your rights to point it out, but avoid prolonged arguments over it for now, since your child needs to focus on their exams. It's a team effort and the family has to pull together and make sure all energies are devoted to the task at hand.

Have meals with the family

Chances are, your child is cooped up in their room for long hours preparing for their exams. Make sure they have their meals with the family, so that they get a break from the monotony of constant studying. Keep the dining table conversation light, so that your child feels refreshed.

Avoid burdening them with your stress

We know you're stressed, probably even more than your child. But when the exam date nears, it's time to back off and let the child be calm. If you're still wracked by nerves, vent to a partner or a friend. Your child is stressed enough and can do without you adding to it.

Make sure they get a good night's sleep

A good night's sleep is very important. Check your child's timetable to ensure they have enough time for a well-earned sleep. This will calm their nerves and keep them alert on the big day.

Keep away from digital distractions

It's difficult to steer clear of digital devices completely, but it's critical to do so during exam time. Install parental controls on your child's devices so that you can ensure they keep away from distractions and focus on doing their best during exams.

Incentives and bribes

There's a fine line between an incentive to do well and outright bribery. Your child should be motivated to put their best foot forward in their exams, without you offering a bribe, such as an expensive gift. However, a family meal or outing is a good idea after the exam as it will also help take the pressure off.

Be a sounding board

Ask them how their exam went, but withhold judgment. Offer to be a listening post, without blaming them for anything they've got wrong in the answer sheet. Be encouraging about the remaining tests and keep them hopeful about the outcome. Let them know you're there to fofer support, whatever the outcome.

Be available

Make time for your child, particularly during the important papers. If possible, if you have leave left, inform your office and take it during this time so you can be around your child. Stay aware of their needs, whether it's a spot of revision, a cup of coffee to perk them up or just being available to address any concerns.

Maintain a balanced diet and routine

Whether it's the daily glass of milk or almonds, make sure your child isn't skipping meals and is eating on time. Nutrition plays an important role in keeping energy levels up.

CHAPTER FIFTEEN

Examinations are Necessary

Before you start preparing an exam
Why are you giving an exam to your students?

To evaluate and grade students. Exams provide a controlled environment for independent work and so are often used to verify students' learning.

To motivate students to study. Students tend to open their books more often when an evaluation is coming up. Exams can be great motivators.

To add variety to student learning. Exams are a form of learning activity. They can enable students to see the material from a different perspective. They also provide feedback that students can then use to improve their understanding.

To identify weaknesses and correct them. Exams enable both students and instructors to identify which areas of the material students do not understand. This allows students to seek help, and instructors to address areas that may need more attention, thus enabling student progression and improvement.

To obtain feedback on your teaching. You can use exams to evaluate your own teaching. Students' performance on the exam will pinpoint areas where you should spend more time or change your current approach.

To provide statistics for the course or institution. Institutions often want information on how students are doing. How many are passing and failing, and what is the average achievement in class? Exams can provide this information.

To accredit qualified students. Certain professions demand that students demonstrate the acquisition of certain skills or knowledge. An exam can provide such proof – for example, the Uniform Final Examination (UFE) serves this purpose in accounting.

What do you want to assess?

What you want to assess should be related to your learning outcomes for the course.

Knowledge or how it is used. You can design your test questions to assess students' knowledge or ability to apply material taught in class.

Process or product. You can test students' reasoning skills and evaluate the process by focusing the marks and other feedback on the process they follow to arrive at a solution. Alternatively, you can evaluate the end product.

The communication of ideas. You can evaluate students' communication skills their ability to express themselves - whether this is by writing a cogent argument, or creating an elegant mathematical proof.

Convergent thinking or divergent thinking. You can test your students' ability to draw a single conclusion from different inputs (convergent thinking). Or you may alternatively want them to come up with different possible answers (divergent thinking). Do you expect different answers from students, or do you expect all of them to provide the same answer?

Absolute or relative standards. Is student success defined by learning a set amount of material or demonstrating certain skills, or is student success measured by assessing the amount of progress the students make over the duration of the course?

How do you decide what to test and how to test it?

The overall exam should be consistent with your learning outcomes for the course. There are a number of ways to review and prioritize the skills and concepts taught in a course. You could:

Use the topics list provided in your course outline

Skim through your lecture notes to find key concepts and methods

Review chapter headings and subheadings in the assigned readings

What are the qualities of a good exam?

A good exam gives all students an equal opportunity to fully demonstrate their learning. With this in mind, you might reflect on the nature and parameters of your exam. For example, could the exam be administered as a take-home exam? Two students might know the material equally well, but one of them might not perform well under the pressure of a timed or in-class testing situation. In such a case, what is it that you really want to assess: how well each student knows the material, or how well each performs under pressure? Likewise, it might be appropriate to allow students to bring memory aids to an exam. Again, what is it that you want to assess: their ability to memorize a formula or their ability to use and apply a formula?

Consistency. If you give the same exam twice to the same students, they should get a similar grade each time.

Validity. Make sure your questions address what you want to evaluate.

Realistic expectations. Your exam should contain questions that match the average student's ability level. It should also be possible to respond to all questions in the time allowed. To check the exam, ask a teaching assistant to take the test – if they can't complete it in well under the time permitted then the exam needs to be revised.

Uses multiple question types. Different students are better at different types of questions. In order to allow all students to demonstrate their abilities, exams should include a variety of types of questions. Read our Teaching Tip, Asking Questions: 6 Types.

Offer multiple ways to obtain full marks. Exams can be highly stressful and artificial ways to demonstrate knowledge. In recognition of this, you may want to provide questions that allow multiple ways to obtain full marks. For example, ask students to list five of the seven benefits of multiple-choice questions.

Redeemable. An exam does not need to be the sole opportunity to obtain marks. Assignments and midterms allow students to practice answering your types of questions and adapt to your expectations.

Demanding. An exam that is too easy does not accurately measure students' understanding of the material.

Transparent marking criteria. Students should know what is expected of them. They should be able to identify the characteristics of a satisfactory answer and understand the relative importance of those characteristics. This can be achieved in many ways; you can provide feedback on assignments, describe your expectations in class, or post model solutions.

Timely. Spread exams out over the semester. Giving two exams one week apart doesn't give students adequate time to receive and respond to the feedback provided by the first exam. When possible, plan the exams to fit logically within the flow of the course material. It might be helpful to place tests at the end of important learning units rather than simply give a midterm halfway through the semester.

Accessible. For students with disabilities, exams must be amenable to adaptive technologies such as screen-readers or screen magnifiers. Exams that have visual content, such as charts, maps, and illustrations, may need to be rendered by Waterloo's AccessAbility Services into a format that meets an accommodation.

After the exam is ready

Prepare a marking scheme or rubric

Preparing a marking scheme ahead of time will allow you to review your questions, to verify that they are really testing the material you want to test, and to think about possible alternative answers that might come up.

Look at what others have done. Chances are that you are not the only person who teaches this course. Look at how others choose to assign grades.

Make a marking scheme usable by non-experts. Write a model answer and use this as the basis for a marking scheme usable by non-experts. This ensures that your teaching assistants and your students can easily understand your marking scheme. It also allows you to have an external examiner mark the response, if need be. A rubric can be an effective tool to help you or your teaching assistants assess student work quickly and accurately. Sharing the rubric with your students as they begin to study for the exam is also a good idea.

Give consequential marks. Generally, marking schemes should not penalize the same error repeatedly. If an error is made early but carried through the answer, you should only penalize it once if the rest of the response is sound.

Review the marking scheme after the exam. Once the exam has been written, read a few answers and review your key. You may sometimes find that students have interpreted your question in a way that is different from what you had intended. Students may come up with excellent answers that may be slightly outside of what was asked. Consider giving these students partial marks.

When marking, make notes on exams. These notes should make it clear why you gave a particular mark. If exams are returned to the students, your notes will help them understand their mistakes and correct them. They will also help you should students want to review their exam long after it has been given, or if they appeal their grade.

Inform students of the purpose and parameters of the exam

Clearly communicate with students about what your goals are for any test or exam. Don't assume that students know what the pedagogical purpose of the test or exam is. Have a discussion about your goals and desired outcomes, and help students understand how specific aspects of the test or exam fit these goals. Be open to making some changes if students have ideas to offer.

Point out the important sections in course plans, textbooks, and readings to guide test and exam preparation; where possible, provide multiple samples of tests and exam questions and answers. Consider conducting an exam review exercise.

Although you might not provide students with exam questions in advance, you should be prepared to answer questions such as:

What will the exam cover?

How much emphasis should I put on the textbook / lectures / etc...?

What material (if any) am I allowed to bring into the exam room?

When will I get my mark?

What happens if, for a good reason, I can't attend the exam? Do I get to re-write?

Will I be given the chance to choose the topics on which I do questions?

Will I be told which criteria I am being assessed on?

If I disagree politically or philosophically with the marker, will I get poor marks?

Will allowances be made if English is not my first language?

After your students write the exam

Monitor the quality of your exams

Exams provide you with the opportunity to obtain feedback on student learning, your teaching methods, and the quality of the exam itself.

Write impressions on your exam and keep them. During the exam and the marking of the exam, keep track of which questions seem to be well understood, and which questions were frequently misunderstood.

Collect numerical data. If you have machine-scorable exams, you can get statistics on your questions, such as which questions were missed most often or which distracters were most often chosen. In other cases you can collect an overview of the marks.

Get student feedback. You can leave space specifically for feedback on exams, or you can obtain feedback in class after the exam. Consider asking your students to complete an exam wrapper – a short survey asking students about exam preparation strategies they used, what questions they found difficult to answer, and what they might do differently to prepare for the next exam (see our Teaching Tip on Teaching Metacognitive Skills).

Why examinations are necessary for students growth

"Exams" – the word itself brings fear among the students. Examinations are a part of life, but for the students, they are a source of anxiety and frustration. Exams have an important role in the process of learning and in the whole educational institution." Exams and tests are a great way to assess what the students have learned with regards to particular subjects. ... Strengths and weaknesses can also be assessed through exams.

Many of the students get irritated when they heard the words of an exam because their exam mentality is very poor, maybe they don't know about the importance of exams.

Generally, students give oral and written exams in their schools/colleges. They have a wrong belief like an exam is not necessary but if they try to think in a detailed positive manner at that time they able to understand the benefits of exams.

Exams are excellent tools to assess what pupils have learned in certain topics. Exams will reveal which parts of the class each student appears to have remembered and shown the most interest in. Exams are also a fantastic opportunity for teachers to learn more about their pupils because each student is unique. The exam atmosphere adds to the tension, allowing teachers to see how their pupils dispute and think independently through their work, which is a valuable trait to remember for future class activities.

Exams can also be used to measure strengths and shortcomings. Teachers will be able to recognize when more class attention is required while teaching a specific subject. When grading the works, a pattern of flaws may emerge. Mock exams are a wonderful method to utilize while teaching before formal examinations in this situation. This will allow students and teachers to identify their deficiencies in time to prepare for the formal exam. This will offer them every one the opportunity to guarantee that they can perform to their full potential in class, which will benefit them in the future.

As you become older, school gets more difficult. As a student, you will grow as a person, and the school curriculum will become more difficult. Exams help higher education institutions to determine if the students applying will be able to meet the job demands. Although the notion of "rating students' competence based on grades" may appear harsh, it is a more efficient approach for them to analyze students' potential, which is especially essential in higher education institutions.

The test process aids the school in determining which faculties and classrooms require additional attention or funding. Exams are a wonderful way to track the development and efficacy of a class. Schools need to make sure that they are providing the finest education possible to their pupils. Based on the grades of the students, school officials can determine where improvements are required within the school, institution, or university. According to studies, a "happier class obtains higher marks," therefore a pattern of comparable average outcomes might suggest whether or not a class is motivated.

After reading about all of the advantages and benefits obtained, it's clear that the worry and ripping my hair out were all worth it in the end. I've identified my talents and shortcomings and applied them to my current situation. I'm beginning to believe that the adage "school is the finest days of your life" is truly true.

Exams and tests are a great way to assess what the students have learned with regards to particular subjects. Exams will show what part of the lesson each student seems to have taken the most interest in and has remembered.

With every pupil being so individual, exams are also a great way for teachers to find out more about the students themselves. The test environment comes with added stress, which allows teachers to work out how their students argue and how they think individually by their works, which is a great attribute for them to keep in mind for future class activities.

Strengths and weaknesses can also be assessed through exams. The teachers will be able to understand where more attention in class may be needed when teaching the particular subject. A pattern of weaknesses may be apparent when marking the works. This is where mock tests are a great technique to use when teaching before the formal examinations. This will give students and teachers the opportunity to understand where their weaknesses may be, in time for the preparation of the formal exam. This will give them all the chance to ensure that they are able to achieve the best of their abilities in class, thus helping them in the future.

School becomes more demanding as you get older. As you grow as a person, you also do as a student and the school curriculum becomes more demanding. Exams allow higher education establishments to assess whether the students applying are going to be able to deal with the work demand. Although this idea of "ranking students capability based on grades" seems harsh, it is an easier way for them to assess the students' potential, which becomes even more important with regards to higher education establishments.

The exam process is beneficial to the school in regards to assessing where faculties and particular classes need more focus or resources. Schools need to ensure that they are offering students the best that they are able to and exams are a great technique to use to monitor the progress and effectiveness of that particular class. School administrators can see where improvement may be needed within the school, college or university based on the students' grades. Studies have shown that a "happier class has higher grades" so a pattern of similar average results may indicate the motivation that a particular class may have or not.

After reading about all the benefits and advantages gained, it just goes to show that the stress, pulling my hair out was all worth it in the long run. I have found my strengths and weaknesses, applying them to where I am now. I am starting to realise that the age old saying "school is the best days of your life" could actually be true...

Types, Characteristics, and Suggestions

Examinations are a very common assessment and evaluation tool in universities and there are many types of examination questions. This tips sheet contains a brief description of seven types of examination questions, as well as tips for using each of them:

1) multiple choice,

2) true/false,

3) matching,

4) short answer,

5) essay,

6) oral, and

7) computational.

Remember that some exams can be conducted effectively in a secure online environment in a proctored computer lab or assigned as paper based or online "take home" exams.

Multiple choice

Multiple choice questions are composed of one question (stem) with multiple possible answers (choices), including the correct answer and several incorrect answers (distractors). Typically, students select the correct answer by circling the associated number or letter, or filling in the associated circle on the machine-readable response sheet.

True/false

True/false questions are only composed of a statement. Students respond to the questions by indicating whether the statement is true or false. For example: True/false questions have only two possible answers (Answer: True).

Matching

Students respond to matching questions by pairing each of a set of stems (e.g., definitions) with one of the choices provided on the exam. These questions are often used to assess recognition and recall and so are most often used in courses where acquisition of detailed knowledge is an important goal. They are generally quick and easy to create and mark, but students require more time to respond to these questions than a similar number of multiple choice or true/false items.

Short answer

Short answer questions are typically composed of a brief prompt that demands a written answer that varies in length from one or two words to a few sentences. They are most often used to test basic knowledge of key facts and terms. An example this kind of short answer question follows:

"What do you call an exam format in which students must uniquely associate a set of prompts with a set of options?" Answer: Matching questions

Essays

Essay questions provide a complex prompt that requires written responses, which can vary in length from a couple of paragraphs to many pages. Like short answer questions, they provide students with an opportunity to explain their understanding and demonstrate creativity, but make it hard for students to arrive at an acceptable answer by bluffing. They can be constructed reasonably quickly and easily but marking these questions can be time-consuming and grader agreement can be difficult.

Oral Exams

Oral examinations allow students to respond directly to the instructor's questions and/or to present prepared statements. These exams are especially popular in language courses that demand 'speaking' but they can be used to assess understanding in almost any course by following the guidelines for the composition of short answer questions.

Computational

Computational questions require that students perform calculations in order to solve for an answer. Computational questions can be used to assess student's memory of solution techniques and their ability to apply those techniques to solve both questions they have attempted before and questions that stretch their abilities by requiring that they combine and use solution techniques in novel ways.

Today Iam trying to change the exam's viewpoint about the importance of the exam and why an exam is necessary.

Why Exam Is Necessary

But the question here arises – Is examination necessary in school?

The answer to this question is a big YES

Exams are a part of growing up, they are really important and necessary when it comes to knowledge testing.

Examinations are not meant for creating a feeling of depression among students, they are meant to create a sense of responsibility among those learners to remember the concepts and present them in the most valuable form.

Confidence:

The exam develops confidence which increases a student's personality in a hard-working manner.

At exam time, students become conscious about their exam performance and they do hard work and try to give the best performance.

When they get good marks they feel happy and their marks help to increase confidence level.

Enthusiasm for competition:

An exam is just like a type of healthy competition for proving more knowledge and skill.

Every student prepares themselves as they participate in the competition and most of them to prove themselves better than other students, they try to get more score and also built a new strategy for reading, they improve their writing skills for better marks.

Self-analysis of own skill:

The exam evaluates the student's ability of learning. It is an effective way to analyze the knowledge of students. It is a measurement of how much they learn and constraint in the study. An exam is for self-improvement.

Often, students take an exam as a career at that time they are very serious about the exams and they prove themselves for their goal and they get the achievement.

Some schools/colleges enhance the student's knowledge by giving them awards and certificate and motivate students to increase their intelligence which is the proud moments of hardworking not for individuals but also it is all about the support of their parents and teachers.

Learning:

Each and every step of life, we face new situations and learn from them.

An exam is a major factor in learning. students learn the lesson of patience, discipline, and leadership through exams.

Exam help to introduce own skill. Exam develops thinking, logic and makes quick decision-making.

Scholarship:

Sometimes, not each parent are capable to provide the best knowledge for their children at that time scholarship is one of the options for students to study.

An exam is one of the gateways to achieve scholarship and study for further higher education.

Easy judgment for teaching:

Exams is an analysis of the student's understanding and grasping power. It is the judgment of how students are capable of their study. Parents and teachers analyze the potential of the study.

1. Strong memory

Examinations develop a strong mindset with a good memory for remembering the contents taught so as to have a lifetime learning of the same.

Question papers make you remember the concepts taught for a longer period of time.

2. Good grades and confidence

With good grades comes the confidence to stand out and show others the expertise you have in your field.

Grades matter as they are a measure of your conceptual understanding, memory power and knowledge you have in your field.

3. Practical implications

When papers are conducted so as to test the practical knowledge of the same, they turn out to be really helpful for the students in the long run as they are tuned to the practical world around them and the need to apply those fresh concepts, enabling the students to develop new ideas and innovate something new and astonishing.

4. Competitive Spirit

Competition is healthy if it is taken in an unrivalled way. The spirit of competition is in itself a way of promoting and developing new ideas. Some practical exams, when conducted, can really improve a child's thinking capability and create an innovative mind.

5. Ability to work under pressure

It is one of the most fundamental quality to develop in a growing student so that they can handle the pressure when they step out in the corporate environment.

With exams, the ability to work and think under pressure becomes primal thus building an important trait for the students to develop over time.

6. With knowledge comes great power

Exams are a way of testing a person's knowledge. It can bring out the best minds and the minds which are filled with extensive knowledge, research and commitment to work.

They are a way to empower a person and give him the power to speak for his knowledge.

7.Time management

Time management is a key to success and in a skill which needs the practice to master. People struggle even after having years of experience in the corporate world to manage their time efficiently.

Exams are conducted in a limited time frame slot so as to teach the growing minds the importance of time.

8. They act as a feedback mechanism for both teachers and students

The efforts of the teachers and the hard work of the students are both reflected in a very appropriate manner through examinations and assessments. At times it gives a clear picture of what you know and what you thought you knew.

Disadvantages of examinations

"As a popular quote goes – "Everything has certain PROS and CONS", conducting exams also has its disadvantages."

Few disadvantages of examinations include –

1. Cramming and not brainstorming

These days conducting examinations has been associated with obtaining a good score on the test rather than assessing the knowledge gained.

Which in turn leads to cramming and later forgetting the content altogether – a very harmful methodology.

Nowadays due to this reason, the knowledge of the students is getting limited only to books and papers taught in schools or colleges for exams.

2. Unhealthy competition

These days exams are taken in a very unhealthy manner with competition being taken personally and way too seriously so as to damage a child's self confidence.

With parents comparing the results of students and friends, leading to the lowering of a child's potential and confidence.

3. Judging a child's ability through mere exam papers

The results of competitions are taken as a measure to judge a child's overall capability and this should not be the case.

Grades can definitely improve the confidence level but on a similar note, the societal impact and overall development of a student both mentally and physically are of utmost importance.

Schools are a student's second home and exams are a way to make them ready for future challenges so they do not give up when they face hardships.
Schools are meant to provide the student knowledge, care, commitment and lessons of life.

We must not forget that the advantages exceed the disadvantages and hence, exams must be taken as a part of a feedback mechanism for the students.

Exams are very important as they train the students like commanders, prepare them for the war ahead wherein they can excel and prove themselves to be a better version of themselves.

As said- "Challenges don't come to break you, they come to make you realize your true potential".

So for the next time, during examinations- Don't panic, Don't stress, Don't fear just Calm down, relax and gear up for this beautiful challenge.

Remember although a sheet of paper cannot determine your future or your capabilities it can definitely enrich you with good respect, knowledge, experience and challenges that lead to growth.

1. Instills discipline

You can say what you want about exams but they do help you to become more disciplined. The fact that you have to prepare months in advance to conquer examinations in the summer can most definitely set you up for the real world. Take this life skill and use it to become successful in the career path of your choice. Discipline is a key trait of all success stories and this routine will guide you and be your knight in shining armour if you want to make it to the top.

2. Gives you the ability to stay focused under pressure

During the exam, you are put under extreme duress to remember pieces of information which you may have learnt at the beginning of the year. Now this takes extreme focus and dedication to remember that far back and to also apply it to the question in hand. If you can take this as a life lesson, you will be well on your way to glory. The top individuals all possess the trait of being calm during the storm and if you can acquire this trait and focus all of your energy into remaining calm, even in the worst of situations, there is no limit as to what you can do.

3. Qualifications you need in life are only acquired through examinations

In your lifetime, you will come to realise that you need certain qualifications to pass a certain stage in the job process. These qualifications will only be under your name if you pass exams. This is a very good reason as to why exams are important. They are the pathway to a job and without qualifications, your career path becomes very limited.

4. Time Management

Time management is a key skill in life and this skill is definitely acquired through the practice of exams. Before the exam, you would need this skill to learn how to manage your time revising. During the exam, you need to learn how to answer each question in a timely manner so that you leave yourself enough time at the end to review your work. In the exam process, time management is integrated every step of the way. This will instill this life skill in you which will dramatically help you to meet deadlines in your dedicated career.

5. Improve Learning

The exam process improves learning and your ability to take on new information. Going through exams will make your brain adapt to being given new information and it will be able to recall facts and figures more efficiently because it is so used to doing so. Being a good learner is most definitely a good trait to have. Some legends claim that they never stop learning. If they put that much respect on this trait, then you should.

We all remember the exam period in schools. The daunting experience of entering the examination hall, finding your name on the exam desk and taking a seat with a booklet with blank paper and unknown questions. The sweaty hand palms and sickness feeling that seems to have made you forget everything that you have been revising for over the last previous few weeks (or in my case few days, I have always been a bit last minute). In all those years of school, college and university I always wondered what the main purpose was for exams. What would this stress achieve later in our lives? Luckily I am able to look into all this and finally learn that the stressful weeks truly are beneficial.

Are Examinations a Fair Way of Testing Our Knowledge?

Many students dislike exams and children of all ages seem to have a diet of more and more exams that they have to take. Coursework is being discredited as a way of demonstrating knowledge as it is becoming easier to plagiarise or even buy coursework over the internet. This leaves exams as the only obvious choice, but do they accurately & fairly test students' knowledge?

Notes